BECOMING ONE FINANCIALLY

Becoming One Financially

Money Management for New Couples

J. André Weisbrod, CHFC

DAVID C. COOK PUBLISHING CO.
ELGIN, ILLINOIS • WESTON, ONTARIO

LifeJourney Books is an imprint of David C. Cook Publishing Co.
David C. Cook Publishing Co., Elgin, Illinois 60120
David C. Cook Publishing Co., Weston, Ontario

Becoming One Financially
© 1989 J. André Weisbrod

Edited by LoraBeth Norton
Cover design by Donna Nelson
Book design by Karen Mulder

First printing, 1989
Printed in the United States of America
93 92 91 90 89 5 4 3 2 1

General situations and examples used in this book are based on real-life circumstances. However, names may have been changed and details altered to protect confidentiality.

This book is intended to be educational and inspirational in nature. Nothing written herein is intended or should be construed as investment advice regarding the purchase or sale of securities or regarding general securities markets. Nor is anything written herein that is intended or should be construed as legal or accounting advice.

Appropriate professional advice should be sought regarding your own financial planning, insurance, investments, and tax matters.

Library of Congress Cataloging-in-Publication Data

Weisbrod, J. André.
    Becoming one financially / J. André Weisbrod.
        p. cm.
    ISBN 1-55513-634-6
    1. Married people—Finance, Personal.   I. Title.
HG179.W455 1989
332.024'0655—dc19   89-2250
                                                                          CIP

Acknowledgments

To my wife, Jill, I want to express my deepest appreciation for your faithful support and love. Your intelligence, wisdom, and commitment are found throughout these pages.

To my children, David, Jaime, and Vanessa—I am thankful that God gave you to us. I hope you will grow up to love Him and be good stewards of His gifts to you.

To the "Glen Eyrie Fellowship," especially George and Marjean Fooshee, Malcolm MacGregor, Waldo Werning, Ross and Linda Kneen, Jerry and Donna Lawson, Howard Dayton, Jim Underwood, Dick Bruso, and Ed Hutka (who have offered special encouragement and support), thank you all for reminding me that there are Christians who have dedicated themselves to financial integrity and sound stewardship. You are sorely needed by the Body of Christ.

To Lin Cook, who persevered with me to get this book published, thank you. Your persistence helped me through some discouraging moments.

To my pastors, John Guest and Chip Nix, and to the congregation of St. Stephen's in Sewickley, Pennsylvania, thank you for providing a Christ-centered body through which I have received many blessings and had the opportunity to develop much of what is included here.

To the engaged couples who have attended our

"Nearly-Wed Retreat" and to those who helped develop it, especially Chip and Carol Nix, Rob and Ginger Stage, Dave and Ann Black, Mark and Cindy Zimmerman, and Bill and Gayle Hess—thank you for your commitment and for sharing your knowledge and gifts so those couples might be better prepared for their lives together.

Finally, to the people of those churches and organizations who have invited me to speak and teach, and to those who have attended workshops and read my newsletter—I deeply appreciate your support, comments, criticisms, and encouragement.

God bless you all.

J. ANDRÉ WEISBROD

TABLE OF
Contents

*To my parents, John H. and Frances A. Weisbrod,
who have provided a wonderful example of integrity,
honor, and love in all areas of their lives,
including the way they handle money.*

Preface

Every day roughly 14,000 Americans get married. Every day almost 7,000 Americans get divorced. Half of those are divorced in three years or less; the average length of the marriages ending in divorce is seven years.

Now, the good news is that half of the couples marrying do stay together. But many studies and surveys of long-term marriages indicate that in only a minority of those are the pair actually "happily" married, still in love and intimately united in a growing, healthy relationship. The rest stay together because of children, economics, fear, convenience, or just plain habit.

I hesitate to introduce this book with such unhappy facts, because *Becoming One Financially* is a very positive book with a message of affirmation and optimism for marriage. But its impact on your own marriage may be lessened without an awareness of the contrasting backdrop of reality.

Most of us enter marriage with the strong conviction that we are different from those who get divorced; we will always love each other. In no way do I want to diminish such idealism. However, we need not carry our dreams in a shroud of naivete. Our hopes and commitments will be buffeted, confused, and tested by the winds of a fickle culture and by our own inadequacies. If we are going to survive with our ideals intact, we need to recognize that it will not be easy. We need to look for knowledge and understanding that will help us build solid, fulfilling marriages.

It is in this light that I have written *Becoming One Financially.* One of the most predominant precipitators of marital conflict and breakup is finances. My goal is to assist you in building a solid conceptual and practical basis for managing your financial affairs, thereby helping you to avoid many common mistakes and increasing the likelihood that you will be successful in reaching your financial goals. To the extent we succeed here, I know that your relationship will be strengthened in other areas as well.

All that I have drafted herein proceeds from my understanding of the Old and New Testaments, gleaned from over twenty years of full-time and part-time ministry, including formal theological training and study. It also comes from years of professional experience handling investments, insurance, and other financial matters for my business and individual clients.

Whether you are Protestant, Catholic, or Jewish . . . whether you consider yourself a "Bible-believing Christian" or an agnostic . . . whatever your beliefs, I invite you to consider what I have written and see if it makes sense. I have sincerely and carefully composed my thoughts and explanations to be as consistent with biblical principles as possible. Of course, there is room for discussion, amplification, and even disagreement as to applications, and I want to encourage you to think critically so you can grow together in your own convictions and commitment to each other.

To all the married or nearly married couples who read this book, I pray that you will truly become one, bonded by God's love and commitment.

ONE

Of Romance, Marriage, and Money

J ack and Shelly met each other at a party in college. After two years of dating they decided to get married. Like most engaged couples, they were in love, and their future looked bright. They had everything imaginable to get them off to a great start: good looks, good families, good health, good education, good jobs.

Three years later they were frustrated, angry, and ready to split. They argued about everything, especially in-laws, careers, and money. With the encouragement of their pastor, they agreed to get professional counseling to see if their marriage could be saved.

Prior to marriage, Jack and Shelly had spent thousands of hours learning how to sail boats, play tennis and golf, ski, cook, speed-read, and paint. Jack had undergone years of extensive education for a career in accounting. He also trained from junior high through college to play football. After college Shelly had purchased a computer and taken three years of night courses to enhance her marketing career. *Yet the total of their education and training for marriage was two one-hour sessions with their pastor and a few isolated bits of advice from parents and friends!*

At the root of many marriage problems is the glaring fact that few couples are ever trained to be married. Think

about it: two people enter the most significant and important relationship of their lives with virtually no preparation. We give them a "bon voyage" party, hoping and
praying that their marriage will work out all right. Then
the unsuspecting couple, with little else to go on, embarks
on their journey assuming that it will, indeed, work out all
right. After all, they reassure us, they're in love.

This is a bit like buying a sailboat for two people who
have never sailed and can't swim, taking them to the sea
and, after an hour of instruction, telling them to sail across
the ocean. After all, they like water and think sailing would
be fun. . . .

The Deep Six

Among the most often mentioned precipitators of serious
stress and conflict in marriage are (in no particular order)
sex, careers, health, in-laws, kids, and money. It is rather
difficult to envision a marriage that doesn't encounter
some rough waters in at least one or two, if not all, of these
categories, which I call the "the deep six." Serious, unre-
solved conflict in any one of these areas indicates a significant problem in the relationship.

For Jack and Shelly, the key stumbling blocks were
careers and money. After three years of marriage, their
finances were a mess. They had no savings or investments,
no personal insurance, and no home ownership. They had
put thousands of dollars of purchases on credit cards.
Much of their furniture was financed, and though they
"owned" two expensive cars, they owed more on them
than they could sell them for.

The serious trouble began when Shelly was offered an
outstanding job opportunity at a twenty percent increase
in salary. The only catch was that it was in another city. But
she figured that Jack would be excited, too, because it was
such a great opportunity. He should be able to find another job easily, and he had always supported her career.

But Jack's reaction was negative. They had just settled
down and made lots of friends, he argued, and he was in

the best possible position for his own career. He liked things as they were.

Shelly wasn't about to give up. "But we could use the extra money. I'd be making almost $30,000!"

"Look," he said, "we make over $50,000 between the two of us right now; that ought to be plenty."

That's when the money argument took over.

"But just last week you were complaining that we aren't ever able to get ahead, there's too much on the charge accounts, and you don't understand where all the money goes."

"Well, if you wouldn't use credit cards like they were golden egg-laying geese, maybe we could save something."

"I'm just getting things I need," she protested. "Besides, you wanted the BMW as much as I did!"

"But I don't understand why you can't be satisfied with what you've got!" His voice was starting to rise. "We don't need the extra money!"

Smiling, she shifted her attack. "Maybe you're just jealous that I'd be making more than you. Is that—"

"No! I resent that!"

"Don't get defensive about it!"

"I'm not defensive!"

Soon they were arguing about whose parents provided the worst money-management example, about working wives and children, and about who wasn't adequately fulfilling whose sexual needs.

Jack and Shelly's spending habits and decisions were largely a carryover from their affluent family life-styles, reinforced by their peers. Neither had been knowledgeable about their parents' financial affairs; everything had been provided and, if they had wanted more, they had always been able to find jobs to earn some extra money. When Shelly went off to school, her father gave her a credit card.

While each knew about the other's career goals, they had not anticipated or discussed the time commitments involved or the issue of who would be the primary breadwinner when they decided to have kids, something they vaguely agreed that they wanted "sometime." Both had fallen into a me-first, want-it-now, "Yuppie" life-style.

Hearts and Treasures

Jesus was devastatingly perceptive and powerfully practical about human relationships. One of His teachings was that "where your treasure is, there will your heart be also" (Matthew 6:21). Simple and to the point. We know that the heart was Jesus' primary concern, and in this verse He clearly links economics with the heart. Therefore, economics is clearly a priority for Jesus.

Money, careers, credit cards, homes, transportation, food, clothing: all of life is economic exchange within relationships. Even sex is economic, in that it is an exchange of energy, emotion, and time between two people. This is the way God created His universe, as a synergistic and symbiotic economic system of relationships. God wanted us to be interdependent on each other and on the creation.

Even in Eden there would have been exchange of goods and services. I can imagine a conversation something like this:

"Yo! Eve! What say I pick some melons down the hill while you grab some peaches from over there, and we'll share."

"Sounds great, Adam. While I'm at it, maybe I'll look for something new to eat."

There you have it. Need, demand, supply, division of labor, energy expended, energy replaced, relationships developed. Bingo! The first economy!

Marriage is the most intimate of economies. Two people merge their lives together in permanent commitment. Therefore, finances should be among the most important areas of concern in our marriages.

But to help couples understand and handle their financial affairs, I find it important to deal with the marriage relationship as a whole. Becoming one financially is dependent on the entire mix of personalities, beliefs, experience, education, and skills you bring to your relationship. It is a lifetime process of commitment and exchange.

TWO
Promises, Promises

"Daddy?"

"Yes, David?"

"We go see planes?"

My two-and-a-half-year-old son and I were on our way to the construction site of our new house. As usual, the excitement of Greater Pittsburgh International Airport had captured his attention as we drove by. Since we did not need to be back for a couple hours, I agreed. "Sounds good. We'll go watch the planes after we look at our new house."

We had great fun climbing over piles of dirt, peering in the windows, and scaling the back hill to view the whole neighborhood. It hadn't seemed to take much time, but when we returned to the car, I realized we had just enough time to make it back home so I could get ready to go out with Jill that evening. I hustled David into his car seat and began the drive home.

I drove along the familiar route on some sort of autopilot—driving safely and accurately, but with my mind focused on other things. Suddenly David pierced my absentness with a great weeping and wailing.

What happened? Had a bee flown up his shorts? Something surely was wrong, but as a hurt or angry two year old is not the most articulate communicator, I couldn't understand his anxiety.

"What's wrong?" I hollered.

With great emphasis, inflection, and volume, but without diction, he told me.

I tried again. "David! Stop crying and tell me what's wrong. I don't understand."

He was a little calmer now. Between breaths and sobs, I caught a few words: "Air . . . we do . . . go . . . plane . . ."

Plane! The airport! I had forgotten all about it. Now I understood. I had driven right by it, after I'd promised him we would stop. I had also promised Jill I would be back by five-thirty, and I knew I couldn't keep both promises.

Realizing that Jill understood my failures much better than David could at that moment, I turned around and went back to the airport. Thankfully, Jill was understanding, and we made it to our engagement that evening "fashionably late." But the impact of that afternoon caused me to reflect more soberly about the dramatic effect my words, and especially my promises, had on my relationship with my son. How important, really, is a promise?

Broken Promises

It is natural to trust. My son provided ample demonstration when, at the age of two, he stood five or six risers up the staircase, announced to whoever was there (even a total stranger), "Catch me!", and then flung himself into the air, absolutely certain that he would be caught.

If our natural inclination is to trust, it is reasonable to assume that the assault on trust began with some broken promise early in our lives. Your dad promised he'd come to your school Christmas concert, then he had to work late. Your coach promised you would start the next game—and then you found yourself on the bench when the starting whistle blew. Your best friend told that secret she promised never to reveal. It may have been something we would consider insignificant today, but that broken promise was the beginning.

As we grew older, examples of unfaithfulness crowded our innocence and made the darkness of suspicion, cynicism, and hypocrisy part of our daily lives. Never again would we have the natural faith of a child.

You may be wondering why I am including a discourse on promises in a book about finances. The reason is this: becoming one in your finances is a direct result of the commitment and trust you offer to each other.

People marry because they love one another, and they express that love in commitment. That commitment is expressed most clearly in the form of promises. If you are about to marry or have done so recently, I am sure that you believe your marriage to be full of promise. And indeed it is. It is full of promise because it is full of promises.

To the Israelites of the Old Testament, spoken promises and vows were the most serious elements of any relationship. A promise, even a verbal promise, was contractual in nature; breaking a vow could result in the death penalty. A man's word was foremost among his possessions, not treated lightly as in our culture, where even written contracts are regularly broken with little thought or conscience.

The vows spoken at most weddings are both a commitment and a promise. In Christian marriage, the commitment and promise are not just between husband and wife; they are made to God as well.

Relationships are formed because of various factors, including physical attraction, social and financial status, and personality. But without the trust born by promise and demonstrated commitment, such relationships remain shallow, weak, and easily broken.

Marriage is a covenant, the ultimate in contracts; it is not an avocation to be done on a trial basis. The vows of the ceremony make that adequately clear. This is "for better or worse," "in sickness and in health," and "till death do you part."

Kept Promises + Completed Commitments
= Real Love

For many years a pastor and his wife experienced relatively smooth sailing in their marriage. They were healthy, lived in comfortable though modest homes, had children, and enjoyed each other's company.

Then the pastor experienced a deep depression. He

was no longer the pleasant and supportive person he once had been. He didn't understand it, his doctors didn't understand it, and his wife surely didn't understand it. He was unhappy and unproductive. This was not what he or his wife had envisioned marriage to be like. And this was no passing, temporary mood—it lasted fourteen years!

All through those years, the pastor's wife stayed with him and tried to help him and support him. I am sure there was a moment or two when she wondered if it was worth it, or if she might be happier somewhere else with someone else, but she did not throw in the towel.

After fourteen years, the pastor came out of his depression. What followed were a half dozen wonderful, productive, and fulfilling years of marriage and ministry.

Then the pastor's wife developed cancer. Now the pastor focused his attention on her. He returned her love, and as she had given herself to him, he gave himself to her until she died.

This was no fair weather love, no mere affection or attraction that retreated in the face of difficulty. These two were special among God's people, an example to us of the special love God has for us and that we can have for each other.

Jill and I have witnessed other examples of such love—a marriage where one partner developed multiple sclerosis, yet the marriage did not fail, another in which one partner had an affair, but the other did not give up, and prayed and persevered until the marriage was restored. These are just a few examples of the real, for-better-or-worse kind of love—God's kind of love. In all of these, the power of promise and commitment overcame tremendous challenges to the marriage.

I recall a quote attributed to Billy Graham's wife. Asked if she had ever considered divorce, she replied, "Murder, yes; divorce, no." Yes, it was a funny quip, but the point is important—not only is marriage not easy, there will be times when it is not enjoyable, either. There will be times when circumstances throw you a great challenge. And there will be times when you let each other down or irritate and aggravate each other to distraction.

The idyllic visions of marriage that we hold at the beginning of our unions are rarely, if ever, the reality experienced. Though Jill and I have not faced tests as severe as those mentioned above, the substance of our marriage has not gone unchallenged. There have been rough times where either or both of us have struggled with our feelings and the longings of our hearts. There have been times of weariness with the effort of commitment. But even when our feelings were confused, our commitment to each other has overcome doubt, depression, sickness, and accident.

What Have You Promised?

Perhaps this is a good time to remember what you have promised each other. Have you promised "to have and to hold, from this day forth"? I find this language in the traditional marriage ceremony quite interesting.

In this context, "have" means to receive, to acquire a new relationship. "Hold" could have a number of possible meanings. I believe it is to be used in the sense of sustaining and retaining, as well as "to have the benefit or responsibilities of" and "to remain true" (Funk and Wagnalls).

"From this day forth" can only be understood to mean unending and of a permanent nature. And of course, this is emphasized by the pronouncement that death is the only reason this relationship may cease to be had and held.

Have you promised this holding "for richer and for poorer" and "in sickness or in health"? We have a friend who married a blind diabetic who went through a kidney transplant and significant health-care expense and died at a relatively young age. He was a marvelous person, but he was neither rich nor healthy. His wife acknowledges that their marriage was tough, but she will also affirm that it was good, and that she is thankful for the time they had together. She understands promise and commitment.

The marriage vows were not written with any ifs—to have and to hold if I continue to feel the same way two years from now as I do today, or if my partner still looks good, or if my partner keeps the house clean, or if my partner makes love the way I want and as often as I want, or if my partner makes the right amount of money and progresses in his or her career so we can have the life-style to which I want to become accustomed.

Are you prepared to back up what you have promised? Is your commitment strong enough to withstand the pressures, temptations, and tragedies that can befall a marriage? I don't mean to sound like a prophet of doom, but if you're going to go out for the football team, you should expect to get tackled now and again.

Your Biggest Financial Commitment

Marriage involves a significant financial commitment. For most of us, it will be our biggest. It is not so much that a husband or wife costs a lot of money. In fact, two together can sometimes live more cheaply than two apart. It is that, from now on, your financial decisions need to be made, not just with regard to your own wishes and needs, but with serious consideration of your spouse's concerns.

If you handle your resources without such concern, it will likely be a source of problems in your marriage. Men are more often guilty than women of using money as a way to hold power over their spouses. I know men who virtually keep their wives prisoners by keeping them in ignorance of how much they make, where it all goes, or even how it is managed. The wife is given an allowance, and if she wants or needs something extra she has to beg, seeking the benevolence of the great "macho" man.

Some may be surprised to hear that this is still true, but in spite of the women's rights movement and more career women, such financial serfdom still exists. Unfortunately, you can find a lot of it among conservative, fundamentalist Christians. Many Christian men like to think that Ephesians 5:22 ("Wives, be subject to your husbands") gives them the right to control and relegate their wives to subservient roles.

Such a rationale is profane. Three verses later, Paul exhorts the men to "love your wives, as Christ loved the church" (verse 25). How did Christ love the church? By becoming her most loving and sacrificial servant, even to the point of dying for her. Jesus was and is strong. He was and is the head of the church. He is never domineering.

Financial commitment in marriage involves loving your partner with your money. Both of you are responsible for being good stewards, so both of you need to conceptually and practically be of the same mind and the same activity when it comes to managing your resources.

Nowhere will this become more important than when you decide (or are surprised) to have children. It is estimated that, on the average, it costs between $200,000 and $250,000 to have a child and raise him or her through college. Now I believe a creditable job can be done for less, but the point is that kids cost a lot!

Don't slough it off. Consider your financial promise and commitment to each other with utmost seriousness and careful attention. You will be glad you did.

Individual Exercise

Each of you write for ten minutes.

- What couples do you know who are an example to you of real promise and commitment in marriage? What is it that they have or do that you would like for your marriage?

- What promises and commitments will I make or have I made to my fiance/spouse? Especially, what am I promising financially?

Discussion

After writing, come together to share your responses. There should be no comments or criticisms during this sharing, although you should feel free to ask clarifying questions to make sure you understand what is being said. After each has shared, discuss the following.

- In what ways are your responses similar? In what ways are they different?

- Pick what you believe are your partner's two most important promises to you. Why are they the most important? How do they make you feel?

THREE
Effecting the Merger and Becoming One

A legal commitment to merge two companies is sometimes called a covenant. It is a written contract and public proclamation of a new relationship. The idea is that the two together will become a stronger single entity. The old companies may retain much of their old identities, but usually much will be changed.

Marriage is, in a very real sense, a merger. First, it is a merger of two lives. But it is also a merger of other family members, friends, and cultural backgrounds.

When two people merge their lives in marriage, it is not an ending; it is a beginning. The event is easy. You say, "I do," your partner says, "I do," and you do. But the process is anything but easy. What follows are the key elements in this most special merger process.

Leaving

"Therefore a man leaves his father and his mother."
(Genesis 2:24)

There comes a time in every person's life when he must leave home and be independent. This leaving is not just physical, though that is important. The leaving must be emotional and conceptual as well. It is a leaving in body, heart, and mind.

Leaving is crucial for a healthy marriage. If you are to become one flesh with your mate, there must be a real breaking away from parental control and dependency. The parent-to-child relationship is no more. This is not to imply the end of the connection, but its redefinition; the relationship is now an adult-to-adult or parent-to-adult relationship. It can still be close and loving, but it is different from what it was. When a person remains unhealthily tied to parents, the marriage is likely to suffer.

Make sure you have both left your families. Help each other identify those areas in which the "child" still exists. Discuss them and try to find the right ways to go about leaving.

I take the concept of leaving one step further. I believe we also need to leave our culture, including our friends, in a similar manner. The marriage should be more important to us than old life-styles. Again, this does not have to mean ending those old relationships (though that may be necessary).

The leaving part of the marriage process can affect your finances in many ways on which I will not elaborate here. But I am sure you can understand how a dominant parent or group of friends can influence spending decisions. If you are going to build a new, self-fulfilling economy with your spouse, you need to be able to set aside past and present influences and begin building your financial working principles from the ground up.

Committing

Bacon and eggs can help us understand commitment. Eggs
come from a chicken and bacon from a pig. Now the
chicken was just sharing, but the pig—now that's
commitment!

To become one, a commitment to the covenant relationship discussed in Chapter 2 is paramount. The first phase of commitment is to take the marriage vows. The second phase is the leaving. The third is the working out of the relationships as described in the rest of this chapter.

From a Christian standpoint, this presupposes a basic commitment to Christ, both as individuals and as a couple. The Lord's intimate involvement in your marriage will give you the resources necessary to protect and fulfill your marriage.

Nothing will better help your marriage function well fiscally than a commitment to follow basic biblical principles of financial management. Chapter 6 offers an outline of these principles.

Accepting

"Just as I am . . . I come."

If the ministry of Billy Graham were to be reduced to one statement, I believe it could come from the message of the song sung when Billy asks people to come forward and accept Jesus into their lives. The message is this: No matter who I am, what I've done, or from where I've come, Jesus accepts me, just as I am.

This is grace, and it is the most crucial doctrine of the Christian faith. Without grace, we are truly lost. We cannot be good enough to deserve eternal life, we cannot be smart enough to think our way into it, and we cannot be wealthy enough to buy it. Baptism, communion, the Ten Commandments, worship services, and all other religious accoutrements are worthless without grace.

Just as I am. This is how God in Christ accepts us, requiring nothing more than our turning from being our own gods and accepting Him and the relationship He offers. Interestingly, the Bible uses marriage as a comparison to the relationship between Christ and believers. Regarding becoming one, Paul teaches that "This is a great mystery, and I take it to mean Christ and the church" (Ephesians 5:32).

Far too many of us enter into marriage with the idea that we will change those things we don't like about our mates. Even though it is unspoken and even hidden deep inside, we enter the relationship conditionally, retaining a lot of "ifs" for leverage.

But while both people in a marriage will inevitably change as the relationship grows, the best change is that which is the result of unconditional love, acceptance, and respect. We cannot change our partner's basic temperament or physiology. The most wonderful gift a husband and wife can give each other is unconditional acceptance.

(I am not saying there should never be conditional parts of the relationship. If one partner is continually adulterous or abusive, the other may need to separate himself or herself, along with any children, until the destructive behavior changes. But this does not preclude the acceptance of love. Indeed, according to Romans 5:8 it was "while we were yet sinners Christ died for us.")

We are not perfect. Husbands and wives will hurt each other, fail each other, and irritate each other. To get beyond these faults takes a special kind of love—an accepting, graceful love—the kind of love that comes from God. Within such love, growth and healing are possible. Within such love, differences and conflict can be overcome, and the relationship can improve, growing stronger and more fulfilling year after year.

If one of you has a more spontaneous personality that can result in impulsive spending, acceptance of that fact by both of you is important. Then you can work on ways to control that spending, to change the mechanics of financial management.

What you are saying is, "I love you and accept your spontaneity. In so many ways, your impulses are wonderful and fun, but they can also get you into trouble. Since we both recognize that impulse spending is a trouble area, let's find a way to help avoid situations that encourage that kind of spending."

Assessing

"For which of you, desiring to build a tower, does not first sit down and count the cost, whether he has enough to complete it?"
(Luke 14:28)

Jesus was speaking here about the cost of being one of His followers. The simple practicality of His statement fits many situations, including marriage and finances.

Assessing your marriage is a matter of taking inventory of your assets, both in terms of who you are (temperament, education, skills, etc.) and what you have (property, savings, investments, etc.).

Chapter 9 shows you how to assess your financial resources. I would also encourage you to discuss with your spouse and make a list of your other personal resources (i.e. time, gifts, talents, and abilities). When it comes down to division of labor within your marriage, such discussion is extremely valuable.

Seeding

"Other seeds fell on good soil and brought forth grain, some a hundredfold, some sixty, some thirty."
(Matthew 13:8)

As early in your marriage as possible, plant seeds for that which you both wish to grow, and plant them in good soil.

The tree of fidelity can grow out of the seed of commitment and vows and the good soil of the positive emotional and physical attention you give to each other. The fuller a marriage is with such attention, the less empty spaces there will be for weeds such as infidelity to sprout.

The fruit of healthy, good children grows from the seed of love planted in soil of support, encouragement, instruction, and discipline. The vine of stewardship grows from the seed of tithes planted in the soil of good financial habits, discipline, and planning, fertilized with a strong desire to give.

On a practical level, each financial goal will begin with the seed of money saved and invested in soil that will allow it to grow. This is why a "seeding" plan that identifies specific goals is so important to your financial success. Visualize each dollar of your income as a seed. How much is landing on rocky ground, how much is choked by weeds, and how much is planted properly in good soil?

Weeding

Marriage problems are like weeds; they thrive on a lack of attention.

Anyone who has ever planted a garden knows about weeds. It seems quite unfair that what you really want to grow requires so much attention and effort, while it takes absolutely no effort to grow tons of unwanted things.

The garden of your marriage is going to require weeding. When you see something growing that you don't want in your marriage, discuss it and figure out a way to get rid of it. Some weeds are relatively easy to extract, others have deep roots which cling tenaciously. Some may need professional help. But whatever, don't ignore weeds or they could take over and destroy the garden.

Financial weeds include impulse spending, excess taxation, bad investments, lack of discipline, disability, poor job/career situation, and poor advice. As you are able to identify each as a real weed, dig it out and replace it with good seed.

Growing

"When the divine owner takes possession of a property, he has a twofold objective: intense cultivation and abounding fruitfulness."
Norman P. Grubb

Assuming you have seeded and weeded, you need to water and fertilize properly to provide the best possible conditions under which plants can grow and bear the best flowers or fruit. They must also have the right temperature range and be exposed to the right amount of sunlight.

For our marriages the soil is love, the sunlight is God's word, water is the Holy Spirit, temperature is our attitude and commitment, and fertilizer is experience. Even bad experiences can enrich the soil if we remember and learn from them.

Financial growth occurs through compounded interest, capital growth, and appreciation. Put your assets to work within the framework of good planning, discipline, and sound advice.

Harvesting

"Who plants a vineyard without eating any of its fruit?"
(I Corinthians 9:7)

The time for harvesting can vary, depending upon the type of plant and its purpose. Some plants provide fruit to be eaten. Some provide flowers to be enjoyed and shared. Others provide building materials.

If you seed and weed and provide a good growing environment, your marriage will bear much fruit and the world will be better off for it. You may have children or adopt some. You will help other couples. You will be an example. You may be instrumental in bringing others to Christ. Your marriage will bear good fruit; you will be fulfilled and satisfied.

Financial harvesting occurs when investments and prosperity are used to build a house, pay for an education, provide income in retirement, or provide for others' needs. There will be many moments of harvest during our lifetimes if we have tended our gardens well.

Being

"Stop and smell the roses."

Sometimes the activity of life, even the good things, can overwhelm us. Working, planning for the future, administrating the details—the cares of this world can prevent us from really living today, just being as God intended us to be.

It is good to remember that marriage is something to be enjoyed. Life is an act of being, and sometimes that is good enough. God created us for fellowship with Himself and each other. When our work and activity precludes such fellowship, we neglect our gardens, and the plants may not grow well or may even wither and die. We may even mistake weeds for flowers and fruit trees. Don't forget to enjoy the flowers and fruit of your marriage.

Plan your time and your finances to allow regular focus on being with each other in special ways. While an ocean cruise might be nice, a walk in the park or a special candlelight dinner can do just as much, or more, for your relationship.

Individual Exercise

Each of you write for fifteen minutes.

• How many hours of premarital counseling have you/will you/did you have, either with a counselor such as a minister or in a class or weekend retreat? Do you think this is/will be/was enough?

• Do you believe you have adequately "left" your mother and father as discussed in this chapter and are ready to enter marriage as fully an adult as possible? Have you "left" your friends and culture?

• Do you believe your fiance/spouse has "left" mother and father? Friends and culture?

• If the answer to any of these is no, please explain.

• Are you committed to Jesus Christ? Is your fiance/spouse? Which of you do you think is more mature in the Christian life? Why?

• Do you believe a commitment to Jesus Christ is (choose one) essential/very important/somewhat important/not very important to the health of your marriage? Why?

• If you could change anything about your body, what would it be? About your temperament or personality?

• Is there anything about you that you believe your fiance/spouse would like to change?

• On a scale of 1 to 5, with 1 being "completely" and 5 being "not very much," how well do you believe you accept your fiance/spouse, just as he or she is? How well do you believe your fiance/spouse accepts you?

• What five seeds would you most like to plant and grow as fruit for your marriage?

healthy finances	friendship	children
material security	hospitality	travel
emotional security	freedom	trust
good health	acceptance	fidelity
mutual servanthood	warmth	adventure
fun and good humor	respect	good sex
Christ-centeredness	generosity	excitement
high standard of living	ministry	

Discussion

First, share, without comment or criticism; then discuss your responses to the previous questions.

FOUR

Of Temperament, Culture, and Conflict

Bonnie, an assistant manager for a sporting goods firm, and Jim, who had recently joined a large law firm, began dating in their mid-twenties. Both were making good incomes and had been living on their own for more than five years.

Both had nice apartments which they had gradually furnished themselves. Bonnie had decorated in a very warm manner with some old wood furniture donated by family and some complementary pieces she had bought herself. Jim had done his "bachelor's pad" pretty much from scratch in a more modern motif, utilizing a lot of glass and metal and plastic. Bonnie was impressed by his ability to decorate and keep his apartment looking nice.

Bonnie and Jim spent a lot of time with each other for about a year, and then decided to marry. Some months before the wedding, they began to discuss where they would live. Since Bonnie had a roommate and Jim didn't, he suggested she move in with him after the wedding. That seemed fine with her.

Up to this point, Bonnie and Jim had experienced smooth sailing in their relationship. They had many common interests, and had often remarked to their friends that they never fought. But that night, things changed. After dinner out, they went over to Jim's apartment to relax and watch some TV. During a commercial, Bonnie casually remarked, "You know, my love seat would fit perfectly here, and we could move your couch over by the other wall."

"I think that would make this room too crowded," responded Jim. "I thought we would put some of your furniture in storage and maybe sell the rest. Besides, your love seat really wouldn't look good next to my furniture."

Thus began their first major argument, one that still creates tension after five years of marriage. Bonnie felt Jim was putting down her taste and was totally insensitive to the value she attached to items that her grandmother and parents had given her. Jim thought she was being overly sentimental about some things that were not really all that good looking and wouldn't fit the decor he had imagined. It would really be too "hodgepodge," and he liked coordinated design.

Aesthetics aside, they found themselves locked in battle due to the physical fact that they couldn't fit two apartments of furniture into one. Practically, they were not ready to afford a larger apartment or house. A temporary truce was reached only when Bonnie agreed to let Jim's furniture be temporarily dominant and the rest be put into storage until they bought a house. Bonnie thought it would be a waste to sell such solid furniture ("They don't make tables like that anymore"), which she was sure they would be able to use someday. Jim thought the cost of storage was too high, and they would do better to sell it, invest the money, and later buy new furniture that would be exactly what they wanted.

1 + 1 = (Unh! Mmpfh! Squeeeeeze) 1 (Plus Change?)

People are different. I know, big revelation. But while we know it to be unalterably true, we often fail to accept the fact and live gracefully with the diversity.

Rooms full of tables and chairs are not the only excess furniture we bring to a marriage. When two people marry, they bring with them a history of experiences, habits, and beliefs. They also bring family members and friends. Careers, hobbies, financial conditions, and personal dreams are also part of the package. And don't forget about each other's genetic heritages, which are the blueprints for our bodies and our temperaments.

All these and more combine within individuals to produce what we call personality. This is who we are. Some of it we like. Some of it we don't.

When people are "in love," they tend to view their partners selectively, choosing to see that which turns them on about each other, while minimizing that which turns them off. Perhaps this is good, or we might not have any marriages. But it is important to acknowledge the various "rooms" each brings to a marriage, and begin to deal with them with a mature love and acceptance.

If you or your partner has been married before, you may have to deal with "furniture" from the previous marriage(s), such as financial obligations, children, and multiple sets of in-laws. These commitments and relationships have to be realistically acknowledged and assimilated into the new relationship as constructively and lovingly as possible, or they will amost surely become a source of serious future conflict.

Do not ignore these issues. Talk them over and decide together how best to handle them. Remember, marriage problems are like weeds: they thrive on lack of attention.

Personality and Temperament

Relationships are expressions of personalities and temperaments. The things we think, do, and say are a culmination of many elements that make up who we are. Even the little things, that we know are really insignificant, can still be occasions for conflict.

Do you throw your socks on the floor and leave beard clippings in the sink? Do you leave stockings over the shower rail? Do you scrape the dishes well, or leave stuff to dry and harden in the dishwasher? Do you slowly savor hard candy, or do you noisily crunch it for that burst of flavor?

Some of these habits reveal more about us than we might suspect. Bill, a psychologist friend of mine, suggests that if you are a candy cruncher, you may tend to approach life in a more experiential or existential manner. He tends to be a candy cruncher himself, and explains that other aspects of his behavior are consistent with this side of his temperament.

As a youth, Bill approached his paper route as a challenge. Each day was a race to see if he could set a new speed record or throw the paper farther and more accurately. The money he earned tended to go like his candy, with an intense burst of enjoyment, easy come and easy go. The exception was when he had a specific purpose or goal in mind.

He remembers a time his father promised a special vacation with travel by airplane if the children paid a certain portion. Bill was able to save for this clear objective, but it was not his natural way. Without such high motivational purpose to overrule his existentially oriented temperament, he would not listen to good advice even if he agreed with it. It is something that he has had to work on, allowing the good side of this personality trait to be valued but keeping the negative side from causing too much trouble.

A Closer Look at Temperament

Each of us is born with certain temperamental characteristics. This is neither good nor bad from a moral standpoint. God knew what He was doing when He gave us differing temperaments. Just because some of us approach life with an orientation toward feelings, while others may relate more with thinking and logic, does not mean either is "wrong"—they are just different.

However, it is important to recognize that your temperament has a lot to do with the way you handle your finances. Practically, your temperamental orientation can be a strength or a weakness, depending on what you are trying to do. Where it is helpful, it should be encouraged and utilized; where it gets us into trouble, we need to be able to deemphasize it and control it.

Some very interesting and helpful work has been done in the area of personality and temperament by such psychological researchers as Myers-Briggs and Keirsey. In their book, *Please Understand Me,* David Keirsey and Marilyn Bates have built on the work of Jung and Myers-Briggs, proposing that out of eight basic personality traits (Introversion/Extroversion, Sensation/Intuition, Thinking/Feeling, and Judging/Perceiving), there are thirty-two mixed types and four generally dominant types that can be observed. It is not asserted that people neatly conform to one of these types, only that people's personalities generally tend to be more strongly oriented toward one than another.

For instance, some people tend to be more extroverted while others are more introverted. One person may make decisions based more on feelings while another may make decisions more on thinking. A natural preference for practical thinking based on the senses (facts) marks one type, while another relies more on intuition, imagination, and "big-picture" conceptualization. Some people prefer clear judgments and the settling of things, while others want to perceive open options and process.

Few people are totally one type or the other, but they usually exhibit or emphasize one type over another the majority of the time. Some people will find themselves "on the line," meaning they retain two contrasting types almost equally.

For those who have some misgivings about psychology, please understand that I do not introduce what follows as a replacement for the biblical view of mankind. I include this material because it can help us gain a better understanding of ourselves, which I believe to be very consistent with Scripture. If you have had a bad experience with psychology or psychiatry, or have been taught that these are "worldly" and anti-Christian, I can only ask that you keep an open mind and not chance throwing the baby out with the bathwater.*

1. Sensing-Perceiving

These people tend to be more impulsive and want to have a great deal of freedom and personal control. They do not like to be too confined or obligated. Experiencing and enjoying life today is more important than planning and saving for the future. In money matters, they will tend to be more impulsive in their spending. They dislike budgets, and are less bound by duties and responsibilities. They are more likely to have debt problems, which they will tend to ignore, feeling that today is what matters and tomorrow will somehow work itself out.

If they find a job that fits them, they are excellent and very competent workers. They are doers, but they do something—driving a truck, piloting a plane, shooting a gun, or climbing a mountain—just because they feel like doing it. If life gets too dull, they will create action, even a crisis. If they don't like their jobs or other life situations, they are likely to move on and try something else. In Keirsey and Bates's words, "Resources are to be expended; machinery is to be operated; people are to be enjoyed."

Friends will tend to experience them as full of life, adventure, and fun, the life of the party. They are survivors; setbacks are only temporary, and they will get right back up and try something else, for it is the action, the challenge, and the experience that turn them on. They may become great entertainers and artists, explorers and athletes, as well as construction workers, race car drivers, and pilots. Babe Ruth and Amelia Earhart displayed strong Sensing-Perceiving tendencies, as did the apostle Peter.

They may be at their best, even heroic, in a crisis. But spouses, family, and others—especially those with temperaments that emphasize such attributes as organization, re-

---

*Descriptions of the four personality types which follow are in large part summarized and paraphrased from *Please Understand Me* by David Keirsey and Marilyn Bates, © 1984 Gnosology Books, Ltd.

sponsibility, and duty—will often end up frustrated by these people and sometimes hurt and betrayed. Our culture has generally been more tolerant of men than of women who have strong Sensing-Perceiving temperaments.

II. Sensing-Judging

Judging here is not meant so much in the sense of "judgmentalism" (though there may be some of this), but more in the sense of desiring completion, closure, and fulfillment. Where Perceiving persons are happy with independence, process, and the doing, Judging people tend to be more concerned with the shoulds and oughts of obligation and duty.

These people may have strong needs to belong—to someone, to a group, to an organization. But they do not want to be dependent; rather, they see themselves as givers and aiders. Freeloading is not an acceptable behavior. They will earn their way.

There is a strong sense of hierarchy and tradition for these people. Order, rules, and obligations are the important stuff of life. If they fail in their duties or are unprepared, they will feel significant guilt and failure. Therefore, they try to be more prepared, especially regarding details, because they assume bad things will happen. They are list-makers, and their concern for details may cause them to fail to see the forest for the trees. Former President Jimmy Carter has strong Sensing-Judging characteristics. The apostle Luke might also be placed among this type.

These people tend to be more organized in their financial affairs, especially in the area of record keeping and making budgets. They will also tend to be savers, even to the point of being tightfisted with money.

Keirsey and Bates tell us that we can see much of the difference between Sensing-Perceiving people and Sensing-Judging people by considering Aesop's fable, "The Ant and the Grasshopper." The ant responsibly and dutifully plans and works and saves while the grasshopper fiddles around and then ends up going to the ant to be bailed out when he finds himself in trouble.

Sensing-Judging people tend to be conservators and historians, as well as workhorses in corporations and organizations. Yet they often feel (and often are) unappreciated by those who benefit from their industry and preparation. This, plus their natural pessimism, can lead to depression.

They will often be found as nurses, accountants, middle managers, civil servants, teachers, and administrators. Indeed, one reason many people of other temperaments (especially Sensing-Perceiving and those with strong Intuitive orientations) have trouble with school and corporate systems is that Sensing-Judging people are almost forty percent of the population. They dominate the educational and organizational world in sheer numbers, though they will not normally be the leaders and visionaries that create those organizations.

III. Intuitive Thinking

The Intuitive Thinkers are a minority, approximately twelve percent of the population. Most are extroverted. While the first two major types have lots of their own to surround them, Intuitive Thinkers often feel like aliens, not understood by parents or teachers or corporate bosses who are less likely to be Intuitive Thinkers.

Intelligence and competence are highly valued and sought. They make good scientists because they are interested in understanding, explaining, predicting, and controlling. They will be found as "renaissance" people, having learned, tried, and practiced in numerous vocational and avocational areas competently and often expertly. Most likely, Leonardo daVinci was an Intuitive Thinker, as was Einstein and the apostle Paul.

However, these people may not do well with line-item administration. Once the basic concept or skill is mastered, details may be left out as they move on to other vistas. They will not likely be good accountants.

Intuitive Thinkers often are visionaries, innovative, big-picture people who are concerned with the possibilities of life and knowing as much as they can about it. Mere facts and order are not as important as reasons, strategies, and new possibilities. They may be inventors, architects, or field marshals. They tend not to be content to leave things as they are, but will try to change and improve things. They are great conceptualizers, designers, and planners. They know what should be done, can design a system to accomplish it, but, ironically, are not necessarily good at implementing the detailed activities required to complete a project. In other words, they may not be good administrators.

Their ability to handle money is generally good, especially on the conceptual/planning side. They understand what good money management is and know how to make good decisions. However, they may have trouble keeping good records and making the checkbook balance.

Marching to different drummers, they may be perceived as independent, strange, and rebellious. They approach life differently and are not as much concerned with the established rules and protocol as they are with new ideas and the importance of things. They are often misunderstood as being negative or antiauthoritarian or egotistical when they are only expressing important insights and trying to make things better. They may have a high regard for others and can feel great emotion, but are less likely to show it.

They are extremely self-critical, requiring much more of themselves than they require of others (although others may not understand this). Competence and knowledge can become so important that even play is approached as hard work.

Intuitive Thinkers often have inquiring and open minds, entertaining suggestions and criticism with less defensiveness than others. They also tend to be very straightforward with people. Others, however, may perceive them as being aloof, enigmatic, and even threatening, which is both a surprise and a mystery to the Intuitive Thinkers. They do not show their emotions as easily as others and may hurt others' feelings without intent or knowledge that they have done so.

IV. Intuitive Feeling

Definable, practical, and physical goals are not most important for Intuitive Feelers. These people are more concerned with "finding" and "being" themselves. Theirs is a search for inner fulfillment and meaning. Like Intuitive Thinkers, they are a minority.

They invest themselves with great energy and feeling into relationships and work. Rejection, real or perceived, is devastating. Life is a drama in which meaning and purpose are paramount. They greatly value their own and others' feelings. King David and Joseph (in Egypt) had strong Intuitive-Feeling personality traits.

They will tend to be found in the more "human" professions, such as dramatic literature, journalism, psychiatry, ministry, and teaching. In fact they will be the only other major type, along with the more numerous Sensing-Judging type, to have many of their number be teachers.

Intuitive Feelers want to experience life, much like the Sensing-Perceivers, but they want the experience to be drenched in meaning beyond the experience itself. They are idealistic and emotional. They are more concerned with relationships than with material things.

Their approach to money will tend to be defined within their relationships, and, therefore, may appear inconsistent. They will not be as concerned with planning or budgeting and record keeping, unless it is important to their relationships and their self-meaning. Nor will they be extravagant or undisciplined spendthrifts, though they may be more impulsive when spending is felt to be meaningful to themselves or others.

Variety: The Spice of Life

Now, there are many temperament type combinations, and few people exactly fit one of these stereotypical descriptions. In fact, we should be diligent in avoiding stereotyping people. People are too complex to be so neatly categorized. However, the knowledge of temperament types can give us some insights to the ways people approach life, and the strengths and weaknesses people bring to relationships.

Many people are versatile, having many characteristics from many types. It should not surprise us that Jesus seems to have represented each of the types with considerable versatility. Most people, however, will tend to have one of the temperament types dominate their personality.

It is important to recognize that Jesus' disciples represented many different temperaments. Obviously, this was a source of conflict, but it was also a great source of strength. This has enormous implications for the Church: Jesus not only accepts diversity, He requires it!

Therefore, if you can understand your marriage partner's temperamental tendencies, you may be able to avoid many conflicts and the heartaches they can cause. And more importantly, you will be able to take your differences and weave them into great strength for your marriage, your children, and the rest of the world.

Culture Combines with Temperament

Background and experience can reinforce or retard our natural temperaments. It is virtually undeniable that the culture we live in helps shape our attitudes and beliefs.

If you were born and raised in Iran, it is almost certain that your beliefs, attitudes, and practices would be radically different regarding such issues as religion, marriage, education, and work, than if you were born and raised in Chicago. Race, nationality, geographical location, income, and social class are among the variables that contribute to our diversity as human beings.

What are the cultural factors that combine with our temperaments to influence the way we handle our finances? The first is family. Other key factors include friends and peer groups, job and career situations, religious institutions and groups, education, advertising and promotion, media (books, newspapers, TV, and movies) and economic/financial systems and availability (of products and services). These are the primary "inputs" into our temperaments. A sad fact is that family and church are often overwhelmed by the other influences, which, in concert, exert a most powerful force.

Christians will add two more forces that vie behind the scenes for our allegiance; they are God and Satan. The spirits of good and evil are at work continuously in this world. God wants us to see beyond the influences of this world and make His love the dominant influence of our lives. The enemy wants to use the cultural factors to manipulate our temperaments in such a way as to keep us from God's influence and ultimately destroy our lives.

This is what Paul, the Intuitive Thinker, was writing about in Ephesians 6:12: "For we are not contending against flesh and blood, but against the principalities, against the powers, against the world rulers of this present darkness. . . ." And I am certain it is what he had in mind when he wrote Romans 12:2: "Do not be conformed to this world but be transformed by the renewal of your mind."

To not be controlled by the combined forces of temperament and culture is indeed difficult. This is why drawing strength from a power greater than ourselves is so important to being and becoming all that we know we should be.

Conflict Is Inevitable

Conflict is an inevitable part of marriage, as it is in all human relationships. Married couples who claim that they never disagree either have very poor memories or very boring lives. But not all conflict is a direct result of temperament or culture. For instance, men and women have certain physical differences that result in different approaches to bodily functions.

One night we were awakened by a scream, followed by some rather forceful and angry verbal assaults directed by Jaime at David. Evidently David had been up before Jaime and had gone to the bathroom. Like any reasonable male, he lifted the toilet seat before relieving himself, thus avoiding problems with his mother the next morning. However, he forgot to put the seat back down. When Jaime, in sleepy delirium, approached the bathroom, she failed to check before she sat down and—you know the rest of the story.

Sooner or later (it's usually sooner), every married couple will have to deal with this important conjugal question: is the husband responsible for putting the seat down when he is finished, or will the wife always remember to check to see if the seat is down?

Most often, conflict is born out of a blend of temperament, culture, and circumstance. Indeed, even the story above is applicable only to cultures that use toilet seats. And the reaction to the circumstance certainly recalls temperament and culture.

But we do not need to be slaves of these factors, buffeted and tossed about like a ship with no rudder. We can guide and overrule temperament and culture and control our response to happenstance through our beliefs and wills. Moral and ethical decisions which proceed from clear thought and right motives (i.e., love) can govern our responses to conflict. These do not and should not eliminate temperament and culture. They merely provide the rudders and power with which to guide our ships through troubled waters. For the Christian, the most important power and rudder are provided through faith in Jesus Christ, who gives us access to God's love and power through the Holy Spirit.

Conflict is inevitable. How we meet it and deal with it is the real measure of who we are.

Financial Conflicts

Financial conflicts in your marriage can come from a great variety of sources. Temperament can cause serious conflict. For instance, if a Sensing-Perceiving person who is more impulsive and concerned with life enjoyment in the present marries an Intuitive Thinker, the fur may fly as budgets aren't followed and checkbooks don't balance.

The Intuitive Thinker, who desires a plan and thinks toward the future, becomes frustrated with the Sensing-Perceiving person's impulsive spending habits and lack of foresight. The checkbook is a mess because the Sensing-Perceiving partner doesn't see what the big deal is and just figures it will all work out ("Let's just believe the bank and not worry about it"). The Intuitive Thinker doesn't want to be bothered by the details, but is upset by the failure to do what he knows should be done. Arguments about deficit spending may be a regular and escalating storm in such a marriage.

A Sensing-Judging husband married to an Intuitive-Feeling wife might have good control over the budget and checkbook, but may tend to keep the wife in the dark about their finances and totally dependent on him. There may be little evidence of outward conflict, particularly if the wife does not really want to deal with money matters other than spending it. But she could secretly nurture a deep resentment because of his control. If he is disabled or dies, she may be completely at a loss about the family finances, not knowing how much there is, where it is, or what to do with it.

To some people, money means security or power or status. In his counseling, my friend Bill sees people using money in many ways. He has talked to husbands who exercise undue control over the money to exert dominance over their wives, and wives who spend to get even, even scheduling lots of expensive therapy to "get" the husband where it hurts—in his pocketbook.

Even in an age of feminism, it is common to find women who are very insecure and fearful concerning financial matters. Not that you won't find men who are insecure and afraid; it is just more prevalent among women. Culturally, many women have been put in a passive, dependent position concerning money.

Family influence is often a strong source of conflict. If you grew up in a home of loving generosity and financial openness while your spouse grew up in an atmosphere of tightfisted secrecy, it may be hard to shake those traditions and the feelings associated with them. If your parents were free-spenders who had debt problems, you may have learned some of the same habits which got them into trouble. Parental expectations can also exert financial pressure on a marriage, especially when the outward signs of material success and security are the focus.

Jill and I were both fortunate to have parents who exercised excellent control over their resources without being Scrooges. Debt was avoided; credit cards were not treated like cash and were paid off each month. Saving was very important. Keeping up with the Joneses was not.

The key to dealing with conflict is your ability to understand and accept your partner just the way he or she is, not to make it a project to change his or her basic temperament. Look at each other's strengths and weaknesses realistically and develop ways to use both of your gifts to the advantage of your relationship. This is grace, the same grace that God has extended to us in accepting us just as we are, "while we were yet sinners" (Romans 5:8).

If each of you is assured that your partner really loves you and accepts you, warts and all, you will have a base from which to cope with conflict. You will be able to discuss things and find solutions to problems. Together you can mature in your strengths, becoming more and more the people God intends for you to be.

Individual Exercise

Each of you take about ten minutes to write responses to the following:

- Of the four basic temperaments described, which is most like you? List some of the traits that made you select this particular personality. Which is least like you? With which type do you think you have the most conflict?

- In which area or two areas (pick no more than two) do you think you and your fiance/spouse will or do experience the most conflict and stress? Why?

Careers	Children
Finances	Sex
In-Laws	Health

• In which financial area or areas do you think you and your spouse/fiance will be least likely to experience conflict? Most likely?

Spending habits	Budgeting
Giving	Record keeping
Saving/investing	Use of credit/loans
Planning for future	Desire for luxuries
Checkbook balancing	Who makes final decisions
Other _____	

• Do you think your parents were good, bad, or neutral role models in their handling of financial matters? How did they teach you about money?

• How do you think your culture most negatively affects you regarding money and possessions?

Discussion

First share your responses with each other, offering no comment or criticism. Then discuss your thoughts and feelings to your partner's responses in an accepting and graceful manner.

This is not the time to put on the boxing gloves. If there are differences that can't be resolved right now, that's okay; you have a lifetime to work on them. Move on to the rest of the book, because what you find there may help.

FIVE

What Do We Really Want, Anyhow?

The needs or wants of the consumer are called demand.

If you are in your mid-thirties or older, you may remember a commercial from the early 60s for a cereal called Maypo. When the kid screamed, "I want my Maypo!" that was advertising reducing demand to basics. At least that's what the sponsor hoped would be the case: all those kids (and, therefore, moms) out there would demand Maypo.

Of course, necessity can be confused with want. We needed food. We even needed cereal. However, we did not need Maypo!

With due respect to purists in the ad industry, many an ad is designed only to create a want disguised as a need, which can be terribly confusing for those who don't want what they need to want and end up wanting what they don't need more than what they do need. Perhaps we need to ask ourselves regularly, just what do we really want, anyhow? Are we spending our money on legitimate needs, or have we been so overwhelmed by cultural seduction that we are—excuse me—left wanting?

Consider Figures 5A and 5B at the end of this chapter. This chart is designed to help you think through and prioritize what you desire. It is important to distinguish between those things you need and those things which you merely want.

Figure 5A is an example of how someone might prioritize needs and wants. (If you disagree with the placement of some items, that's okay. The idea is to get you thinking.) The further left you go, the more vital the items. As you move to the right, the items take on less and less importance.

In other words, the chart guides you to make distinctions among what is essential, what is important, what is deferrable, and what is really valuable. Do you need what you want? What is the difference between needs and wants? Are your priorities in order? It may not be as clear as you think.

Figure 5B is your chart. Take a few minutes right now to pencil in as many of your needs and wants as you can think of. There are two blank forms, so each person can complete the chart alone, without discussion. Then get together to compare and discuss.

In many cases it may not be easy to decide in which column an item belongs, but do your best. For maximum benefit, do this now, before reading further.

When you are finished, take an overall look and ask what this might reveal about the way you have been managing your finances. I have found a great tendency among people to take care of much of the first two columns of Needs, but then immediately leap across the page into the Wants columns, often purchasing Low Value Wants first. Sometimes they have not even adequately provided for Essential Immediate Needs before they leap over and purchase Low Value Wants. This is where debt problems often begin.

The idea is to begin in the far left column and take care of everything in that column before moving to the next. Everything in a column should be accounted for before allowing yourself to move on to the next column. Now, that might not mean you have completed the purchase; it may merely mean you have figured how much it will cost, how much you will have to save each month to reach your goal, have set up a savings or investment account, and have begun making the necessary deposits.

Much of your financial success or failure will depend on how well you can resist the temptation to jump to the right before you have taken care of what is on the left.

I will deal with the problem of debt in a later chapter. However, it should be noted here that you should avoid the temptation to go into debt. With few exceptions (one being a home mortgage), do not finance your purchases. It is too easy to do and is a black hole which can lead you to financial ruin.

The Bottom Line

The most important confrontation of the Christian life comes when the desires of the heart are examined before the cross. Do we want what God wants? Prioritizing needs and wants is a question of the heart as well as one of clear thinking.

Ask God to create in you a clean heart (Psalm 51:10). Ask Him to help you resist the cultural seductions that would twist you away from what He wants. Realize that your pocketbook is an object of the spiritual warfare described in Ephesians 6. It helps to remember that Satan does not want your money used for godly purposes.

Regarding material desires, perhaps no passage addresses the issue more simply than Proverbs 30:8, 9: "Remove far from me falsehood and lying; give me neither poverty nor riches; feed me with the food that is needful for me, lest I be full, and deny thee, and say, 'Who is the Lord?' or lest I be poor, and steal, and profane the name of my God."

In dealing with your desires, begin each day by asking, "How can I best serve You today, Lord? May I be a blessing to You and to someone else today. Help me to use my time, my talent, and my money wisely. Help me to want what You want." This is a steward's prayer.

FIGURE 5A
Prioritizing Needs and Wants

Needs

Essential Immediate Needs	Important Short-Term Needs	Important Long-Term Needs	Deferrable Needs
FOOD MORTGAGE ESSENTIAL CLOTHING TRANSPORT-ATION REPAIR STOVE INSURANCE/ HEALTH CARE UTILITIES NECESSARY BUSINESS EXPENSES	NON-ESSENTIAL CLOTHING SAVINGS FOR EMERGENCY PAY OFF CREDIT CARD DEBT INVEST IN ED. COURSE FOR CAREER AD-VANCEMENT FAMILY RECREATION & EDUCATION HOSPITALITY FOR FAMILY & FRIENDS CHRISTMAS GIFT SAVINGS	CHILDREN'S EDUC. FUNDS VACATION $$ SAVINGS FOR CAR REPLACEMT SAVINGS FOR APPLIANCES REPAIR/REPLACE SAVINGS FOR DOWN PAYMT ON LARGER HOME SUPPLEMENTAL RETIREMENT SAVINGS SAVE/INVEST TOWARDS FINANCIAL INDEPENDENCE	EXCERCISE CLUB MEMBERSHIP WEEKEND RETREAT BIGGER HOME NEW KITCHEN TABLE

Wants

High Value Wants	Medium Value Wants	Low Value Wants
DINING ROOM TABLE PERSONAL COMPUTER	SECOND CAR VCR SNOWBLOWER PAVE DRIVEWAY SPECIAL VACATION TO DISNEY WORLD	WATERBED EXCESS "LUXURY" CLOTHING EAT OUT MORE OFTEN GARAGE DOOR OPENER

FIGURE 5B

Prioritizing Needs and Wants

Needs

Essential Immediate Needs	Important Short-Term Needs	Important Long-Term Needs	Deferrable Needs

Wants

High Value Wants	Medium Value Wants	Low Value Wants

FIGURE 5B
Prioritizing Needs and Wants

Needs

Essential Immediate Needs	Important Short-Term Needs	Important Long-Term Needs	Deferrable Needs

Wants

High Value Wants	Medium Value Wants	Low Value Wants

Individual Exercise

Fill out the chart (Figure 5B) as instructed in the text. Couples, do it separately first. No cheating, now.

Discussion

After completing the charts, share them with each other. Explain why you placed certain items in certain columns.

- Which areas do you think you have under control?

- Which areas do you think you need to work on most?

SIX

Christian Principles for Financial Management

In the early 1970s, I was employed in full-time youth ministry with Young Life. I owe much to the experiences, knowledge, and wisdom provided by this outstanding international organization, and my life has been enriched by the many wonderful people who became part of my life through it.

But this is not to say that everything was perfect—there were many difficult and trying times. Around 1973 or 1974, it occurred to me that whenever there were organizational and personal problems, money seemed to be involved. Sometimes it was obvious and at the center of a problem, such as when donations ran short and we were not paid for months at a time. Other times it was more subtle, such as when a staff person was hurting and ineffective because his spouse was tired of not being able to provide better clothes for their kids. Often tensions and problems came back to some financial issue.

The ministry could not exist without economic considerations. People could not exist without them. I began to wonder if economics was perhaps at the core of human relationships.

Then I began to wonder why, if this were so, was so little time and attention spent to study and teach economics among Christians. Indeed, it seemed like the only time Christians talked about money was when they wanted some. Stewardship was synonymous with fund-raising, and somehow that just didn't sit right with me.

What was wrong? Hadn't anyone given this much thought? Didn't the Bible have anything to say on the subject? There had certainly not been much emphasis on economics in my seminary courses. I had to assume that either the Bible was silent on the matter, or an awful lot of Christians were missing or ignoring what it did say.

I found out later that others were having similar thoughts—people like Larry Burkett, George Fooshee, Malcolm MacGregor, Waldo Werning, and Ron Sider.* But at that point in my life, I had not been exposed to that minority of Christian thinkers who recognized that stewardship was among the most neglected and misunderstood issues that the church had to face, and that it was also among the most important.

That was when I found a "new" book. Although I had read the Bible from cover to cover, and much of it countless times, I found that it suddenly spoke to me with a new freshness and vitality. Everywhere I turned I discovered economic principles. Passages I had read hundreds of times bombarded me with new ideas and perspectives. Why hadn't I seen it before? Because I had never really considered it or never even bothered to ask if there was much to learn about financial matters in the Bible, I had not noticed much.

This conviction about stewardship, and a sense that God wanted to lead us financially, eventually led us out of nonprofit ministry and into the business and financial world. What I have seen and learned in the fifteen years since only confirms that those early thoughts were good and right.

What follow are thirty-two "working principles" on

---

*Some may be surprised to see Ron Sider mentioned. While I do not agree with everything Ron has written regarding economic systems and solutions, I appreciate his courage in bringing very important issues and concerns to our consciousness. Christians in the United States are in sore need of some compassionate conscience. The day we forget the poor, we forget Jesus. There can be no other interpretation of passages such as Luke 4:18-21; Matthew 25:40; and I John 3:17, 18.

which I base my view of economics and finance. But more than that, these are principles for total living. For that is what stewardship is all about—the appreciation, care, and management of life and creation. Anything less is a misunderstanding of the concept. I find that, when presented in straightforward simplicity, it is difficult to argue with the truth and wisdom of these principles. Indeed, they not only make sense, they work. Try them out and see if you will not be better off for it.

With each principle, I have provided some references with which to begin your own search of the Bible. You will find that most of these principles can be found in the Book of Proverbs, which is where I started. However, they are also found in other books in both New and Old Testaments. The references I have provided are not exhaustive; you will be able to find more if you look.

1. Sincerely seek God's will and His righteousness.
Proverbs 15:16; 11:23; 15:8; 16:8; Psalm 37:25, 26; Matthew 6:1-4, 33.

2. Be thankful.
Psalm 92:1; 95:2; 100:4, Ephesians 5:20; I Thessalonians 5:18.

3. Honor God with your "first fruits" and tithes.
Proverbs 3:3-10; Exodus 22:29, 30; 23:19; 25:2; Leviticus 27:30; Deuteronomy 14:22 and ff.; 16:17; Malachi 3:8-11; Matthew 23:23.

4. Check your desires and motives; seek not your own glory, and avoid the "I wants."
Proverbs 11:18; 13:25; 15:16; 23:4, 5; 30:8, 9, 15; Matthew 6:1-4, 19-21; 16:26; 19:16-24; I Timothy 6:8-10, 17-19; James 3:13-18.

5. Carefully set your priorities; know what is truly important and what is right and wrong.
Proverbs 3:13, 14; 15:16; 24:3; Lamentations 3:40; Micah 6:8; Romans 12:9; 16:19; I Corinthians 14:40; Philippians 4:8; I Thessalonians 5:21.

6. Do not be conformed to this world.
Proverbs 13:7; Romans 12:1,2.

7. Put your trust and obedience in God as your provider;
do not trust in your own skills.
Proverbs 11:28; 28:25; Leviticus 26:3-12; Deuteronomy 8:18;
15:4, 5; Psalm 37:3; 44:3, 6; Job 31:24-28; Jeremiah 29:11-13; II
Corinthians 1:9; Philippians 4:6, 19; I Timothy 6:17; Hebrews
13:5, 6.

8. Hard work can produce value, while sloth and laziness
destroy.
Proverbs 6:6-11; 11:27; 12:9-12; 14:23; 18:9; 20:4, 13; 24:33, 34;
28:19; 30:25; I Thessalonians 4:11; II Thessalonians 3:8-12.

9. Seek quality and excellence in what you do and buy.
Proverbs 22:29; Philippians 1:10; 4:8.

10. Integrity and faithfulness come before wealth.
Proverbs 11:1, 3; 10:9; 22:1; 24:6; Psalm 37:16; Matthew 25:21;
Luke 16:10-13; I Corinthians 4:2; II Timothy 2:2.

11. Treat others (spouse, family, employer, employees,
customers, etc.) honestly and fairly, with concern and love,
in matters of economic exchange.
Proverbs 11:1; Leviticus 19:35, 36; Numbers 30:2; Psalm 62:10;
Jeremiah 17:11; Matthew 7:12; I Timothy 5:18.

12. Take care of your family.
Proverbs 11:29; 15:27; 17:1; 28:24; I Timothy 5:4, 8.

13. Be of one mind with your spouse when making financial decisions.
Proverbs 31:10, 11; Genesis 2:24; Malachi 2:13-15; Matthew
12:25; John 17:21; Ephesians 5:21-33; Philippians 2:2.

14. Remember the poor and seek justice.
Proverbs 14:31; 19:17; 21:3, 13; 22:9, 16, 22; 28:27; 29: 7, 14;
31:9; Deuteronomy 15:4; Matthew 23:23; Luke 4:18-21; Matthew
25:40; I John 3:17.

15. Be generous, a "giver in search of needs."
Proverbs 3:27; 11:24-26; Matthew 10:8.

16. Seek guidance from competent and wise advisers who hold to the same basic values and principles as you do.
Proverbs 11:14; 15:22; 20:18; 23:6; 24:6; Psalm 1:1-3; Ephesians 5:15; Colossians 3:16.

17. Plan and budget with care and prayer.
Proverbs 13:16; 16:3; 21:5; Psalm 127:1; Luke 14:28-30; I Corinthians 3:10, 11.

18. Avoid debt.
Proverbs 6:1-15; 11:15; 17:18; 22:7, 26; Romans 13:7, 8.

19. Do not cosign for the debt of others.
Proverbs 6:1-5; 11:15; 17:18; 22:26.

20. Do not envy those who have more than you or covet what they have: be content with what you have.
Proverbs 23:17; Exodus 20:17; Psalm 37:7; Philippians 4:11; I Timothy 6:9-11; James 4:1-3; Hebrews 13:15.

21. Live modestly; be neither a spendthrift or pleasure seeker. (A modest life-style does not mean "poor." It has little to do with the amount of wealth one has. Rather, it has to do with how that wealth is displayed and used.)
Proverbs 21:17; 30:8, 9; Matthew 6:25; I Timothy 2:9; 3:8; 6:9-11; Hebrews 13:5; James 5:1-6.

22. Be careful of uncontrolled appetites (power, career advancement, status, alcohol, drugs, pornography, gluttony, etc.) which can lead to financial ruin.
Proverbs 21:17; 23:20, 21; Matthew 6:19; Luke 12:15; I Timothy 6:9-11; II Timothy 3:1-5.

23. Be disciplined and in control of your finances.
Proverbs 25:28; I Corinthians 9:25.

24. Consider your risks and protect against them.
Proverbs 14:15, 16; 27:12; Ecclesiastes 5:13, 14; James 4:13-17.

25. Save and invest on a planned, regular basis.
Proverbs 6:6-8; 13:11; 21:20; Matthew 25:14-30.

26. Do not be fearful or timid.
Matthew 25:24-30; II Timothy 1:7.

27. Avoid "get rich quick" schemes.
Proverbs 20:21; Ecclesiastes 5:13, 14.

28. Be an owner of assets of real value (take dominion).
Proverbs 21:20; Genesis 17:8; 48:4; Psalm 8:6.

29. Make what you have grow for greater use.
Proverbs 13:11; 21:5; Matthew 25:14-30.

30. Use money wisely to win friends for God and yourself.
Proverbs 19:4; Luke 16:9.

31. Pass these principles on to your children.
Proverbs 22:6; I Timothy 3:12.

32. Leave an inheritance to your children.
Proverbs 13:22; Numbers 26:53; 27:7-11; Psalm 25:13;
I Chronicles 28:8; I Timothy 5:8.

SEVEN

Three Key Decisions

1970 was a turbulent and uncertain time in history. We had seen a lot in a short few years: the assassination of Martin Luther King and Bobby Kennedy, the Chicago Seven, racial turbulence, campus riots, the Kent State shootings, "grass," "hashish," "speed," and "acid," cults, free love, the assault on traditional values and assumptions.

It was against this backdrop that Jill and I, eighteen and barely twenty-one respectively, were married. The odds were against us. The divorce rate was already about fifty percent, and even less optimistic for couples as young as we were.

Then the idealistic but unsubstantial revolution of the 60s mutated into the materialistic and hedonistic self-indulgence of the "Yuppie" generation. The search for truth and justice and a better world was swallowed in a seeking after something called "self-fulfillment."

I ask myself why my marriage has not only survived but has also grown, when so many forces were aligned to destroy it. True, Jill and I had both made commitments to Jesus Christ, yet that was no guarantee of success. We have seen many couples who shared Christian commitment break up.

Jill and I loved each other. That may sound obvious, but many people enter marriage because they are infatuated with their partners or sex or even marriage itself. Many do not understand the distinction between love and infatuation; for the most part, we did, and that certainly helped. We were and are sexually compatible, and we enjoy each other's company. Our basic attitudes about money and life-styles are the same.

But the first and overriding answer to our enduring marriage is God's grace. Our love has not ceased, even during tough times. We have made mistakes. We have hurt each other. But through it all our basic commitment remains. We are serious about our marriage, and God has given us the grace and strength to keep that commitment at its center.

One area in which we have had relatively few conflicts is that of finances. At the beginning of our marriage, Jill and I made three basic decisions about finances that have helped us avoid many of the common problems we see around us. If you adopt these at the beginning of your marriage, I believe you, too, will see many benefits.

Important Decision #1: To Tithe

First, we decided to tithe. How much easier it was for us to start out with the tithe built into our budget before we developed financial commitments and got accustomed to a life-style! How difficult it would have been to have committed ourselves to mortgages and car payments and accustomed ourselves to designer clothes and luxurious travel and then tried to tithe!

This is why it is so hard for many people to tithe; once they are used to something, it is hard to give it up. But you are not as likely to miss that which you do not have. Life-style will not have become too habitual and material attachments will not be as likely to obstruct your stewardship for God if you have started out right in the beginning.

I would encourage you to tithe, not because I or anyone else does, but because God wants you to. Refer back to Chapter 6. Look up the references for the firstfruits and tithes (principle #3). While the tithe is not a legalistic requirement for Christians, it is nevertheless a crucial part of God's distribution network, and is instrumental to the depth of our relationship with Him.

Jesus endorsed it in Matthew 3:23, and it is also considered a sign of the highest respect and personal commitment in Hebrews 7:5-10. The practice of the Firstfruits Principle comes with a promise in Proverbs 3:9, 10: "Honor the Lord with your substance and with the first fruits of all your produce; then your barns will be filled with plenty, and your vats will be bursting with wine." Interestingly, the tithe is only a part of the firstfruits concept, which even includes children.

To the best of my knowledge, the tithe is the only subject in the Bible on which God specifically challenges us to test Him. "Yet you are robbing me. But you say, 'How are we robbing thee?' In your tithes and offerings. . . . Bring the full tithes into the storehouse, that there may be food in my house; and thereby put me to the test, says the Lord of hosts, if I will not open the windows of heaven for you and pour down for you an overflowing blessing." (Malachi 3:8-10)

We do not offer the tithe to get rich; it is not a magical get-rich scheme. We tithe so that our relationship with the Lord becomes fuller and more in concert with His will. Try it and see if your relationship with God does not grow.

Important Decision #2:
To Manage on a Cash Basis and Not Go into Debt

Our second decision was to spend on a cash basis. If we did not have the money, we were not going to spend what we did not have. The only credit card we had for quite some years was for gasoline. We traveled a lot, mostly hauling kids around as part of our ministry, and it was not always feasible or wise to carry large amounts of cash. And if the van broke down, the card was an important emergency tool. But we were committed to paying off the balance every month and rarely paid any interest. This practice served us well, and we were able to avoid debt problems during our years of full time-ministry, even when we did not get paid for months at a time.

Important Decision #3:
Not to Spend Unless Both of You Are in Full Agreement

Our third decision was not as conscious as the first two; it just sort of happened at first and later became more of a clear working principle that we continue to practice today. We do not make major purchases unless we have discussed them first and are in agreement about them. (What constitutes a "major purchase"? We define it as anything that costs much more than twenty-five dollars and is not in the regular budget.)

If one wants to buy (or sell) and the other does not, the one who wants to buy will wait. We believe that if it is right, the other will come to agree, without manipulation or coercion.

There have been times when we both agreed on something that ended up being a mistake, but we are confident we did not make as many mistakes as we could have had we not practiced this method of mutual trust and accountability.

Discussion

• How do you feel/think about these three decisions?

• Are they decisions you would like to make part of your marriage?

EIGHT

What Is Financial Planning?

In the past, only relatively wealthy people sought or needed wholistic financial advice. Then came the 1970s, with its barrage of volatile economic conditions. Inflation, stagflation, recession, and job insecurity meant that the simple old products of the past—passbook savings, non-interest-bearing checking, traditional mortgages, whole life insurance, long-term bonds—were no longer sufficient.

When inflation and, soon thereafter, interest rates reached double digits, people with passbook savings and long-term bonds found themselves moving in reverse financially. With inflation at ten percent and above, a person in a five percent savings account was losing as much as seven and a half to ten percent in purchasing power (see Figure 8A).

FIGURE 8A
Condition of Passbook Savings Account, 1974-75

Annual gross interest rate	5.0%
Less taxes (50% bracket)	-2.5%
Less annual inflation rate	-12.0%
Real rate of return	-9.5%

Similarly, a retiree who had bought a long-term municipal bond which paid five percent in the early 1970s found himself losing purchasing power; prices of everything went up while his income stayed the same. But when he called his broker to see what he could do to get a higher interest rate, he found that he could only sell his bond for less than two-thirds of what he had originally paid for it. (After all, who would buy his five percent bond at 100% of its maturity value when a newly issued bond gave nine or ten percent?)

Such conditions spawned a whole new era in financial products and services for middle-income people, heralded by the advent of the money market fund in the early and mid 1970s. All of a sudden, lower-income consumers had access to a tremendous array of sophisticated financial tools. The financial industry responded to consumers' demands for more competitive products that would give higher returns and tax advantages in an inflationary, volatile marketplace. Stock mutual funds regained favor, gold was allowed to be sold in a free market, limited partnerships reduced their minimum investment amounts, banks devised greater varieties of deposit accounts and new kinds of mortgages, while insurance companies repackaged term life and whole life into universal life and other variations of life insurance.

The problem, however, was that the proliferation of choices grew faster than the knowledge of most people, resulting in confusion and abuses within the industry. This led to the question of where to get good advice. Out of such an environment came a new term, "financial planning." Financial planning is now the fastest growing area of the financial services industry.

Ten Steps Toward Successful Financial Planning

Financial planning is a process, not an event. A financial plan is not an isolated act; it is a constantly changing series of evaluations and decisions spanning your lifetime. A plan is meant to be changed, of course, but you cannot change what does not exist.

1. *Seek professional help.*

Some people are capable of doing more for themselves than others. This is true in financial planning, just as it is in plumbing, medicine, law, or TV repair. However, the adage correctly asserts that the lawyer who represents himself has a fool for a client. Even trained planners need other financial professionals with whom to confer regarding their own financial affairs.

You may take a very active and directive role, using your financial planner as an expert consultant. Or you may wish to take a more passive role, entrusting your planner or other adviser with greater responsibility for recommendations and decisions.

I must caution you that people can call themselves financial planners whether they have any real credentials or not. Anyone practicing financial planning should have earned one of two respected professional designations, ChFC (Chartered Financial Consultant) or CFP (Certified Financial Planner). If your planner does not hold such a designation, he or she should be currently enrolled in one of these programs and should be closely supervised by someone who does have sufficient credentials.

In addition, you should inquire about experience and other qualifications, as well as the background and qualifications of others in the firm. Find out how the business is handled, how the planner gets paid, and what his or her philosophy is regarding investments, taxes, insurance, etc. Ask for references.

If the planner is also a convinced and committed Christian, that can be a tremendous advantage, in that your planner may be better able to identify with you and understand your goals and values. On a number of occasions, clients have expressed relief that I will help them give away assets when their accountants, attorneys, or other advisers discouraged charity, even calling it foolish. However, do not sacrifice competence. I would rather deal with a competent and honest non-Christian than a Christian who is poorly trained, has the wrong motives, or is just not suited to be in the business.

It is usually an advantage if a planner works in a firm that performs a variety of financial services and employs many qualified experts in different areas of the financial world. Access to knowledge and experience are important.

A financial planner may also be an insurance agent, stockbroker, attorney, or accountant. In fact, most financial planners sell products (investments and/or insurance) or other services (legal or accounting) to survive. There is nothing wrong with this, as long as it is fully revealed up front. Remember, your advisers need to be paid for their work just as you are paid for yours.

I recommend that you shop for brains, not products. If you find the brains, then place your business there. Do not expect to get good, loyal, long-term advice and service if you take the good advice and abuse the adviser by not paying for it.

2. *Take inventory.*

Imagine that you are a woodworker and you have just been commissioned to build a set of custom display cabinets. You know that you will need certain tools and quantities of materials, but in order to know what to order, you first need to know what you currently have on hand. So you spend some time checking to see if you have all the right tools, along with the right bits, wood, hinges, nails, and glue.

Financial planning also requires taking stock of your current situation. The more detail you can provide, the better. Erroneous information can create potentially disastrous results.

For example, I had a client who entered into a fact-finding questionnaire a $100,000 face value for a life insurance policy. When I asked to see the policy, he replied that he couldn't find it, but he clearly remembered that it was $100,000. We contacted the insurance company to double-check the information and learned that the policy was only worth $50,000.

If we had determined his need for life insurance based on the wrong information, and he subsequently died, his family would have been $50,000 short. I don't know many families who could easily weather a $50,000 death benefit shortfall.

Many people believe they have more and/or better

insurance protection than they actually have, especially in the area of group disability insurance. (In many cases, group policies are worth little because the definition of disability is very restrictive and/or benefits are offset by other sources of income.)

An accurate inventory is the proper starting point in the financial planning process. Chapter 9 will walk you through a basic inventory that will be sufficient for most newlyweds.

3. *Define your objectives.*

Financial planning without objectives is like an archery match without a target. If you are to succeed financially and become the steward that you should be, it is imperative that you think through your financial objectives clearly and honestly. It is here that the value of a qualified and competent financial planner will become evident.

Because your objectives will drive the rest of the planning process, you and your planner should define and quantify them as accurately and realistically as possible. Chapter 11 deals with defining your objectives.

4. *Review your basic budget.*

Addressing the issue of cash flow allocation is a never-ending, yet very important, part of your planning. If you spend every dollar that you make, no amount of goal setting or planning will be able to do much for you. Therefore, it is imperative that you budget money for insurance, savings, and investments. Chapter 10 offers a budgeting guide that should get you started well.

5. *Review your taxes.*

Depending on your income level and the complexity of your affairs, this may or may not be much of a priority. Many newlyweds' affairs are so simple that little help will be needed. However, it may be helpful to keep in mind that, under current tax law, there are a limited number of basic ways the typical individual or family can save taxes. These include:

Deductible expenses—business expense (unreimbursed), home mortgage interest and points, medical expenses (unreimbursed), and charitable gifts.

Deductible investments and benefits—retirement plan contributions (pension, profit-sharing, 401[k], IRAs, and others), group insurance paid by employer.

Tax-free income—municipal bond interest, life insurance proceeds (and cash value gains if not surrendered), disability insurance benefits if policy personally owned, certain scholarships and fellowships, up to $500 investment income in child's name.

Tax deferral—life insurance cash value buildup, deferred annuities, retirement plans, and capital gains.

There are other tax-saving strategies that you may be able to employ if you own your own business or when you accumulate a lot of assets and are in the highest tax bracket. This is when a good tax accountant and/or attorney and financial planner should be consulted.

6. *Review your will(s) and estate plan.*

It is estimated that about two-thirds of the adult population die intestate (without a will). And, though I have not been able to confirm this from an authoritative source, I once heard an expert in estate planning reveal that half of all attorneys die intestate!

Among those who do have wills, many of the wills are out-of-date and will not accomplish what the decedents would have wanted. It is important to understand that if you die without a will, the government will make one for you, resulting in additional estate settlement costs and the possibility that your assets will not end up where you want them. Chapter 15 will help you consider the place of a will in more detail.

7. *Review your insurance needs.*

Insurance is the only financial tool that allows you to use a relatively small amount of money to leverage a large amount of money to be delivered to you, your family, or your business if unplanned bad things happen.

A good personal and/or business plan pays careful attention to risk management. It is, most simply, a process of asking "what if" questions. What would be likely to happen if I died? What would happen if I were injured or sick and could not work? What if there were a fire that destroyed my home or business? What if my key employee died? What if my partner died or was disabled?

A financial plan is based on the assumption that you will continue to have your job, your health, and life. However, many people have their livelihoods, their health, or their lives taken from them prematurely. Those who fail to address such possibilities in their planning are playing a kind of Russian roulette with themselves and their loved ones. For Christians and non-Christians alike, such events are a reality.

Nobody likes insurance until they need it, or until someone tells them they can't have it. I have spent many hours trying to find insurance for people who have developed health problems. Invariably they say that they wished they had bought the insurance years before when they could have obtained it cheaply. For those who become uninsurable, the financial reality of their lack of insurance can be devastating. So be sure you and your planner pay significant attention to your need for insurance. Bad decisions here can destroy all your other plans.

A planner is trained to accurately identify and quantify your risks. Where you have insufficient resources to self-insure your risks, insurance policies can cover many of them. Insurance planning is one of the most important parts of the financial planning process and should be addressed prior to investments. Chapters 12 and 13 contain more information regarding insurance planning.

8. *Develop a plan for savings and investment.*

Your savings and investment strategy begins with your objectives, which were defined in Step Three. Typically, basic objectives will include such items as retirement income, children's educations, buying a home, starting a business, buying a car, and general "financial independence."

You will now need to work out numbers that will tell you how much you would need to save and invest at given rates of return to reach your goal. Here you may need some professional help. During this part of the process, you will begin to consider the various investment alternatives that could be suitably used to reach your goals. See Chapter 13 for more discussion on savings and investments.

9. *Implement your plan.*

A few years ago, I did some planning for a man who needed disability insurance. In spite of my strong recommendation and his agreement that he should buy some, he wanted to think about it some more.

Two weeks later he had an accident and seriously hurt his back. He was laid up for a couple of months. Fortunately, his was not a permanent injury. However, he now had a back problem history that meant he would have to pay a lot more for disability insurance.

I talked to another person and recommended that he and his partners review the insurance they had on each other for a buy-sell agreement. I suspected that the policies, which were old, were too small to provide adequate compensation, and I wondered if each of the partners had his personal affairs ordered. He agreed that it was a good idea, but he and his partners were just too busy right then. He suggested I keep in touch.

Two months later one of the partners died. It was then they found that not only should they have had more insurance, but the ownership and beneficiary designations on the old policies were written wrongly, causing legal problems.

The message is clear: everything we have talked about to this point is virtually worthless if you fail to act upon it. A complete discussion of implementation is offered in Chapter 14.

10. *Review your plan periodically.*

Most people should review their plans in detail annually. A review should cover any changes in your personal situations (e.g., new children, an inheritance, a pay raise), changes in general economics and market conditions, insurance, and the progress of your investments. As you and the world around you change, your financial plan will need to be adjusted.

No plan is perfect. Some things will go better than expected and some will be worse. You, your planner, and your other advisers must work together to minimize problems and maximize successes. Regular reviews help you to measure progress and avoid problems.

NINE
Where Are You Now?

Imagine waking up to find yourself on a street corner in an unknown city in a country where people spoke a language with which you were not familiar. Unless you possessed an inordinate amount of poise and self-confidence, you would probably feel very insecure.

The first thing you would want to do would be to find out where you were. Without an accurate idea of your location, you couldn't decide where to go next or how to get there. It would be most helpful if you could find someone you could trust who knew your language and could act as a guide.

For many people, financial management is a good bit like this. Their knowledge of the language is limited, and they are not sure where to start. Others have some knowledge, but are afraid to trust any of the "natives." And, of course, there are some who figure they are smart enough and need no guide, and barge ahead down whatever road seems good to them at the time. They may or may not arrive at a satisfactory destination.

An accurate assessment of where you are is essential if you are going to manage your resources effectively. Figuring out where you are financially is a threefold fact-finding process.

Three Steps to Understanding
Where You Are

First, you need to make a list of everything you own and everything you owe. This is called a net worth statement or balance sheet. You also need to make a list of personal information and other documents and financial products that will not show up on your net worth statement. (These include categories such as homeowners [or renters] insurance, auto insurance, wills, trusts, names, birth dates, and social security numbers.)

Second, you need to know where your income goes. This is the record of current spending (not to be confused with a budget, which is a plan for future spending).

Third, you need to make an objective assessment of your current income and your future income potential, given your background, education, and career choices. This is called the income assessment.

To get started, clear your desk or table. The more surface area you have, the easier it will be to lay things out so you can see them. Gather together the following:

-all investment records and statements
-all insurance records and policies
-employee benefit statements and records
-wills and trust documents
-mortgage statements
-credit card and other loan statements and information
-check registers
-tax returns
-any other records that have bearing on your financial affairs.

If you lack any information, make phone calls or write letters to those who have the information and ask for copies. Once you have gathered all the pertinent data, you are ready to begin.

1. *Taking inventory and making a net worth statement*
Using Figure 9A and Section I of the form at the end of Chapter 13 as a guide, write down all pertinent personal information. If you have personal situations or informa-

FIGURE 9A
Personal Data

NAME: JACK AND JANET NEWLY-WED   DATE 10/3/88

ADDRESS: 24 EAST BAY DR., APT. 34   CITY LOOKAHEAD   STATE PA   ZIP 15200

         YOU: JACK   SPOUSE: JANET

DATE OF BIRTH 7/12/62   S.S.# 189-24-xxxx   D.O.B. 11/4/63   S.S.# 190-16-xxxx

	YOU	SPOUSE
EMPLOYER	ACME DISTRIBUTION CO.	XYZ CORP.
EMPLOYER ADDRESS	2046 PROSPECT COURT	1 ACCUMULATION CENTER
	GIVALOT, PA 15100	GIVALOT, PA 15100
POSITION/ OCCUPATION DESCRIPTION	SALES REP.	COMPUTER TECHNICIAN
AN EARNED INCOME	$29,000	$19,000
HEALTH CONDITIONS	NONE	NONE
PARENTS NAMES/AGE	GEORGE & BRENDA NOSALOT	FRED & JUNE LEVELHEAD
BROTHERS/ SISTERS	JEFF, SUSAN	NONE

IMPORTANT PEOPLE (NAMES, ADDRESSES, PHONE NUMBERS)

ACCOUNTANT   NONE

ATTORNEY   NONE

BANKER   LOOKAHEAD NATIONAL BANK

CLERGY   REV. PIE USNESS

EXECUTOR OF ESTATE   NONE (NO WILLS)

FINANCIAL PLANNER/CONSULTANT

INSURANCE AGENT(S)   COLE ISHUN (AUTO) 642-8888

INVESTMENT ADVISER(S)/STOCKBROKER(S)   NONE

PHYSICIAN(S)   DRS. STICHEM AND HOWE

OTHERS (Children's Guardians, etc.)   NONE

LOCATIONS: ORIGINAL WILL(S) ——   TRUST DOCUMENTS ——

     SAFE DEPOSIT BOX LOOKAHEAD NATIONAL BANK   OTHER ——

tion that could affect your planning, such as chronic health conditions, list them under "other information." On another page, list your insurance policies, including group insurance provided by your employer. (See Figure 9B and Section II of the form in Chapter 13.)

Next, make your net worth statement, using Figure 9C and Section III of the form in Chapter 13 as a model. List the current market values and balances. Where the exact value is unknown, make as reasonable an estimate as possible. Add up your total assets. Then add your total liabilities. Subtract your total liabilities from your total assets. The answer is your net worth.

2. Making a record of current spending

Though budget counseling is not part of my business, many people have come to me for help in this area, many of whom have found themselves with a significant debt problem. Their typical complaint is that they can't make ends meet. Frequently I hear the lament: "I just don't know where it all goes!"

The daily pressures of schedules and commitments in a fast-paced and often frenetic world can sap so much of our awareness and energy that we seem to have little time to think and reflect until after we have spent. We know we started out with ninety dollars cash a couple days ago, and now are surprised to find only twelve dollars in our pocket. Where did it go?

I usually ask the people who come to me with this problem to write down their monthly expenses. Then I ask them to tell me what their monthly take-home pay is. After comparing the net income and the listed expenditures, I often end up asking, "Where's the missing money?"

At this point I usually get a surprised look.

"What do you mean, 'missing money'?"

My observation is that they have listed less in budget expenditures than their net income, and I point this out to them. With further thought, they may come up with a few more items they forgot, but often there is still some "miss-

FIGURE 9B
Specific List of Insurance and Investments

INSURANCE POLICIES

NAME OF COMPANY	POLICY OR ACCT. #	PRODUCT NAME/TYPE	BENEFITS	CASH VALUES
HITANDMISS NATIONAL	4328931	AUTO INS.	LIABILITY & COLLISION	NONE
JACK GROUP		HEALTH INS.	MAJ. MED. 200 DED., 80/20 CO INS. 1st $5000	NONE
" "		LIFE INS.		NONE
JANET GROUP		LIFE INS.		NONE

INVESTMENTS

NAME OF COMPANY	ACCOUNT NUMBER	PRODUCT NAME/TYPE	BENEFITS	VALUE
LNB	43245	CHECKING	——	1,215
LNB	82345	SAVINGS	5½%	2,894
LNB	80262	SAVINGS	5½%	9,872

PROPERTY

PROPERTY NAME/DESCRIPTION	LOCATION	VALUE
1986 OLDS CUTLASS		6-7,000
1987 CHEVETTE		6-7,000

Assets, Liabilities & Net Worth

Name: JACK AND JANET NEWLYWED Date: 10/3/88

OWNERSHIP:	SELF (JACK)	SPOUSE (JANET)	JOINT	OTHER	TOTAL
ASSETS					
CASH/CHECKING			1,215		1,215
SAVINGS ACCTS.	9,872	2,894			12,766
MONEY MKT. FUNDS					
CDs					
STOCKS/BONDS					
MUTUAL FUNDS					
STOCK OPTIONS					
IRA ACCOUNT(S)					
KEOGH ACCOUNT(S)					
VESTED PENSION(S)	2,458				
EMPLOYER THRIFT					
LTD. PARTNERSHIPS					
ANNUITIES					
HOME					
OTHER REAL EST.					
PERSONAL PROPERTY	8,500 (CAR & MISC.)	10,000 (CAR & MISC.)	12,000 (FURNI-TURE, ETC.)		30,500
LIFE INS. CASH VALUE					
BUSINESS INTERESTS					
OTHER					
TOTALS (A)	20,830	12,894	13,215		46,939
LIABILITIES					
MORTGAGES					
PERSONAL NOTES					
CREDIT CARDS					
1) VISA			1,320		
2) MASTERCARD		450	210		
3)					
UNPAID TAXES					
JACK AUTO LOAN	2,400				
JANET AUTO LOAN		6,900			
TOTALS (B)	2,400	7,350	1,530		12,360
NET WORTH (A) - (B)	18,430	5,544	11,685		34,579

ing money," sometimes hundreds of dollars monthly. Now a small miscellaneous category is fine, but when it amounts to five or ten percent of net income, it signals that a spending problem probably exists.

For many, what I am going to recommend now is something you equate with diabolical torture. I realize that it is not easy and may go against your temperament. I don't expect you to enjoy it; however, if you can bring yourself to do this, you may just find it to be the difference between success and failure in reaching your financial goals.

Purchase a little pocket memo book at your local drug or discount store. Carry it with you for thirty days. Every time you write a check, use a credit card, or pay cash, write down the date, a description of the item or service purchased, and the total amount paid. This includes everything, even chewing gum or a can of pop.

At the end of thirty days, add it all up. At least for that month you will know "where it all went."

3. *Assessing your current income and future income potential*

Unless you were born a Rockefeller or have in some other way come into a large sum of money, your ability to earn an income is your most significant financial asset. Whether you are a doctor, a salesperson, or a janitor, your job represents a piece of the economy, an asset which is your productivity. In reality, you are exchanging goods or services with others. You give them time and energy, and you receive time and energy. Money is merely a token or measurement of that exchange.

In general, the relative value of people's time and energy is established by the forces of supply and demand in the economy. Now, we know that there is often great disparity and injustice in that relative value. Christians need to understand that such unfairness is simply one of the many negative results of mankind's insistence on being like God, running our own lives in their own ways, and ignoring His directions for life.

This is what the Bible refers to as SIN, which is not the same as sins. Sins are merely the symptoms of SIN, the logical results of disease. SIN is the condition of being out of relationship with God and running our lives our own ways. For non-Christians, especially those who prefer the label "agnostic," the logic is still applicable: if there is a God, then the world certainly does not have much of a relationship with Him. The injustices of life can only be laid at the feet of a wayward humanity.

I bring this up only to emphasize that we must recognize the imperfections of the economy, adjust to them, and then try to be agents of positive contribution and change. We do this by being responsible stewards, following God's economic principles, and influencing others toward positive change when we have opportunity to do so.

Regardless of your position in the economy, realize that God has a design and place for you in His economy. But in order to be a good steward, you need to have a realistic understanding of how the world's economy values your time, talent, and energy.

List your income today. If you stay on your current career path, what can you realistically expect to earn next year? In five, ten, and twenty years? (See Figure 9D and Section IV of the form in Chapter 13.) Use current pay scales for your type of work. Do not consider inflation here, as we only want to know the relative value of position and length of service for your profession in today's dollars.

This may take some research, but knowing such facts can be a great help in your planning. It may also have bearing on your career choices, though I do not recommend choosing vocations on the basis of what you earn. If God calls you to a lower-paying career because of your gifts, abilities, and temperament, then acceptance of that vocation can make you richer and more fulfilled than anything the world can offer.

At this point you should have a good idea of where you stand financially. You have a "snapshot" of your present financial condition in your net worth statement and spending record, plus you have a reasonably realistic idea of your current income and future income potential. Now you are ready to do some real planning.

FIGURE 9D
Income Assessment

What is your annual income now?	$ *18,000*	
What will it likely be next year?	$ *19,000*	
In five years?	High $ *35,000*	Low $ *25,000*
In ten years?	High $ *45,000*	Low $ *35,000*
In twenty years?	High $ *80,000*	Low $ *50,000*

TEN

Income, Outgo, and Outcome—
Making and Mastering a Budget

When I was a boy, my father would come home at the end of the day and empty his pockets onto his dresser. Keys, miscellaneous items, and paper money were put into a caddie. His change would usually be put into a cardboard box. When the box became full, Dad would take it to the savings and loan, where the coins were dumped into a machine with a rotating wheel that separated and counted them with a great clinking and clanking. I loved to watch the counting machine perform its function.

I didn't think that much about Dad's habit while I was growing up; like most kids, I was too absorbed in my own world. It was not until I was well along into adulthood that it occurred to me—I had attended college, to a great extent, on Dad's loose change!

Dad's discipline was an example to me. Even though for many years his income was not high, and despite periods of financial stress, he had continued to save what he could, even if it was only dimes and nickels.

The Secret to Financial Independence

The secret to financial independence is simpler than you might think—as Samuel Johnson put it, "Whatever you have, spend less." However, though it may be simpler than you think, it is harder than you wish. What makes it work is, in a word, discipline. Without discipline, your chances of achieving financial freedom are slim.

Did you know that many big lottery winners end up broke in a matter of a few years? Did you ever wonder why so many highly paid athletes end up in financial trouble? In most instances, the key reason is a lack of discipline.

Making and following a budget is, without doubt, the most basic of financial disciplines.

The Price Is Never Right

Every couple who wants to be married in our church has to attend a twenty-four hour retreat which Jill and I helped develop. One activity we devised was a game we called "The Price Is Never Right."

Three couples are chosen to be players. By lot, each is given a hypothetical annual income. One couple received $18,000, the next couple $28,000, and the third couple $45,000. Then they are asked to spend their money in typical budget categories, such as food, housing, clothing, vacations, transportation, eating out, etc. In each category, they are given three choices.

For instance, they are shown three pictures of places to live—a modest apartment, a small Cape Cod house, and an upscale condo—and have to choose one.

In the eating-out category, choice one is to eat out once a month at a family-type restaurant with two or three special occasions per year at quality restaurants. Choice two is twice a month at upscale restaurants, and choice three is once a week at quality establishments.

They choose among a used Toyota, a new Olds Cutlass, and a BMW. They decide how much to give to church and charity, where to take their vacations, what kind of food to eat, where to shop for clothes, what kind of insurance to buy, and how much to save and invest.

The couples are told to make their choices with respect to what they think is appropriate for their allotted income. Having researched the cost of the various items and services, we keep a running total for each couple as they make their choices.

We played this game on three different weekends, and not one couple was able to stay within their income! In every case, they overspent and ended up in debt after one year. Ironically, the one couple that came close to ending up the year without a deficit was younger and had been given the smallest income.

Why do we have so much trouble "making ends meet"? I suppose it must be the same general defect which makes other disciplines, such as exercising, dieting, and record keeping problematic for so many. Let's face it; budgeting is easier not to do than to do. And it's not exactly fun.

Making the budget is not really too difficult; it is the mastering of it that defeats us. The key to successful budgeting lies in the commitment to make spending coincide with the budget. Budgeting is only valuable if it is actually used to control spending; otherwise, it is an exercise in futility.

Find the Missing Money

The way to figure out "where the money goes" was described in Chapter 9—carry a pocket memo book and in it record every purchase you make for thirty days.

I have had people tell me that just knowing they had to write down an expenditure caused them not to spend money they would otherwise have spent without thinking. Those last two words are key: without thinking. They had been forced to think and admit to themselves that the expenditure was unnecessary or unhealthy. They were wasting money, and were forced to admit it to themselves.

There are often other "missing" dollars which can be found through attention and good planning. Are there some ways you could save taxes that you are not aware of? Are there ways to arrange your investments and insurance to find some missing money? Whether you are wealthy or poor, you probably have some "missing money" somewhere. See if you can find it and put it to work.

The Ten Percent Solution Model

Most people approach a budget backwards. They put down everything they can think of on which they have been spending money and add it all up, and that becomes their "budget." If there is anything left over, then they may save some of it.

Some people merely figure out ways to spend the excess when they find it. Others do their giving to ministry out of what's left over. Many find their budgets exceed their incomes, and they either try to find ways to cut back or they throw the budget out and hope their problems will go away by themselves.

The place to begin your budgeting process is with a basic conceptual framework. If you are going to be successful in managing your money, you need a system to follow that is understandable, flexible, and adaptable to your situation.

My basic budget model, which I call "The Ten Percent Solution," is such a system. It is really quite simple, but the important thing is that it works. Here is my promise to you: to the extent you are able to follow this model, you will be better off than if you did not.

I want to emphasize that what is presented next is an ideal schematic. Think of it as a target. Some people may be able to adapt their life-styles and budgets to this system immediately, but most people will have to work their way up to it.

If your circumstances are such that you cannot reach the target right away, do not despair. Rather, get excited by the vision and the promise it represents. Once you reach the target, your financial condition (and other aspects of your life) will have so dramatically changed for the better that you will want to reach beyond to even higher goals.

Newlyweds are often in a wonderful position to gain control of their finances because they are starting fresh, often with a clean slate. If you are getting married when you are older or have had a previous marriage, it may be more difficult. How much easier to get your budget control established before you get behind, than to try to unwind years of spending habits and commitments.

Starting at Zero

The Ten Percent Solution begins with a zero base and imposes a basic allocation from which to design the ideal budget for your circumstances. The target allocation system (shown in Figure 10A) starts with gross income (after unreimbursed business expenses) and breaks it down into tenths. The first ten percent is the Lord's tithe. The second ten percent is allocated to savings, investment, and life insurance. The third ten percent is a contingency savings fund to cover unexpected, unplanned expenses. That leaves seven-tenths as an imposed living expense allocation.

Figure 10A
Target Allocation for Cash Flow

Annual earned income $_____

10% Tithe	10% Savings Investment Life Insurance	10% Contingency Fund	70% Living Expense
$ _____	$ _____	$ _____	$ _____

You may be thinking, "There's no way! This is impossible on my income." Remember, this is a target, something definable to set your sights on. Some are capable of achieving or exceeding this target right now. A few may already be doing it and need to think about setting higher targets. Chances are you will need to find a starting point and work up to it.

Consider the example in Figure 10B at the end of this chapter.* Here is a basic, realistic target allocation for newlyweds starting out with a $25,000 annual income.

---

*This example is based on numbers that would work for a couple in Pittsburgh, Pennsylvania, in 1988. Depending on where you live, prices in goods, services, real estate, etc. will vary greatly.

Getting in Shape

If you have ever tried to get in shape for a sport, you know that the toughest part is getting started. Those first few weeks can be agony. You are sore, tired, and wondering if you are crazy for trying. But after a while, your body strengthens. The habit of working out takes hold. The initial soreness and frustration disappear, and you function at a higher level. You feel better, look better—you are better! In fact, once in shape, you will feel bad if you are prevented from working out.

Whether you want to make the Olympics or just get in good enough shape to lose some pounds and feel better, it helps to set targets. The serious athlete continually sets ever higher targets against which he can measure progress; the person who wants just to "get in shape" may set smaller targets, such as a number of push-ups, laps swum, or heart rate attained.

The point is this: without targets, we are less likely to achieve anything, much less know if and when we have achieved it. So don't be scared off from getting into financial shape because it looks hard. Are you satisfied with where you are financially? If not, get started on The Ten Percent Solution now and begin to discover your tremendous stewardship potential.

Take some time right now to fill in the blank target allocation and basic living expense form provided at the end of this chapter (Figure 10C, two copies). I suggest that spouses (or fiances) first do this separately, then compare and finalize. This is a good way to start a very healthy discussion. There is a third copy for your final plan at the end of Chapter 13 (Section VI).

If you want to go into greater detail, you can. You should then keep a record of actual expenses, month by month, and see how close you come to your budget target. This is important to staying in control of your budget.

For self-employed people, I recommend separating business and personal accounts and record-keeping as much as possible. Make separate budgets for business and personal expenditures. Keep a business "capitalization" account (i.e., money market fund) into which all income is deposited. Try to keep two or three months' business and personal expenses in this account. Each month, pay yourself a level "salary." This should help you be more in control of both business and personal finances.

To give you a better idea of the benefits of following The Ten Percent Solution approach, consider the following list of potential results.

The Ten Percent Solution: Results of Disciplined Application

1. Future increases in living expenses can be provided by increased income. Even if earned income does not increase, increased living expenses can come from contingency budget, investment income, or from contingency funds not used in previous years.

EXAMPLE: If $250 per month has been put into the contingency fund and then invested at seven and a half percent, over $10,000 will have been accumulated in just three years. When a large purchase, such as a refrigerator or car, becomes necessary, these funds are available. Debt problems are avoided because disciplined savings provide the funds needed. The point at which all consumer debt can be avoided without invading investment principal or preventing future savings is the point at which financial freedom begins.

For some, this can be accomplished within three to five years. Many should be able to reach this point within ten years. For those with small incomes, large amounts of existing debt or unusual obligations, it may take longer. Regardless, for most people in the United States, it is possible to live debt free and accumulate savings and investments.

2. Additional investment accumulation and increased standard of living can be provided through savings generated by tax-saving devices.

EXAMPLE: $1,000 of savings put into a deductible IRA or 401(k) plan generates $280 of tax savings for a person in a twenty-eight percent tax bracket. That is $280 that did not exist before the tax-saving device was used. Part of the $280 could be put into investment and part could be used to purchase a new kitchen appliance, and/or some could be given away without affecting the rest of your budget.

3. Retirement is provided through employer plans and/or Keogh and IRA plans.

4. Financial independence and inheritance for family and ministry are provided through investments and life insurance.

EXAMPLE: Young newlyweds in their mid-twenties start with an income of $25,000 a year and save ten percent ($208.33 per month) in a contingency fund and put ten percent into savings, investment, and life insurance for thirty years. If we assume their income will increase at an average rate of five percent annually, that cars, a home down payment, future repairs and improvements, some unreimbursed medical bills, and college education costs for two children would be paid out of these funds, then the following could be true within thirty years.

• They would own their home without any debt.

• They would have no other debts.

• They would have approximately $412,000 in various investments which could produce almost $33,000 in annual income at eight percent.

Without house payments, and without an exorbitant life-style, they would be able to provide basic living expenses on their investment income alone, financially independent by their mid-fifties! And this does not consider additional retirement income that would come from company pensions and social security.

5. Protection against loss of income due to job loss or disability (accident or sickness) is provided by accumulated savings and investments and by disability and health insurance.

6. Additional current giving can be accomplished by tithing on realized investment income, tax savings generated by financial planning, and contingency funds unused at year end. This is a way to give more than the basic tithe without eating into your living expense budget.

7. Additional future giving can be provided through creative estate planning, tax planning, and life insurance.

8. Those who have the gift of making a lot of money can set their targets higher. Would it not be wonderful to be able to live off thirty percent, save and invest ten percent, put ten percent into a contingency fund, and give away fifty percent? There are those who are doing this and more.

Regardless of your present situation, the important thing is that you must start somewhere. I do not know who first said it, but it is apropos: "It's hard by the yard, but it's a cinch by the inch."

The idea is to think big, but start small. Whatever you do, do it in faith right now; God will bless it. Remember the boy with the bag of fish 'n' chips that was sufficient to feed 5000? Or the widow's mite? In God's economy, whatever we have is sufficient when it is properly used and offered to Him out of devotion.

It Works!

From a purely practical standpoint, even if your goals are not reached all the time, you will be better off for having done something positive in the right direction. A perfect example was given to me by newlyweds who had heard me talk about The Ten Percent Solution on our engaged couples' retreat.

They shared with me that, since the retreat, they had been tithing and had committed to the ten-percent contingency and ten-percent savings, investment, and life insurance components and had successfully reached their goals for most of about six months. They also bought an older house during this time which, unknown to them, had a problem which required a new roof. This, in turn, wiped out most of what they had saved. But instead of being discouraged, they were thankful. As the woman pointed out, had they not practiced The Ten Percent Solution, they would not have had the money to pay for the new roof; they would have had to borrow the money. They still intended to continue their savings and investment plans. They saw that it worked and knew it would be the key to their financial freedom.

Another young man who had attended our Nearly-Wed Retreat a couple years ago recently thanked me for teaching The Ten Percent Solution system, especially the idea of the contingency fund. Of particular note was his statement that "on December 26, Christmas was over, really over." There would be no trail of debt into the next year, because all had been bought with cash.

These examples are just two of many that illustrate why The Ten Percent Solution budget model is so powerful. Things rarely work out exactly as planned. The discipline of the system gives us a much greater ability to not only provide for our futures and help others; it helps us to meet unexpected difficulties from a position of financial and spiritual strength.

Essentially, this is what Joseph did to meet the needs of Egypt. He anticipated hard times and, with God's direction and understanding, practiced the principles of saving, investing, and insuring. (Read Genesis 37—45, especially 41:33-36, from a financial perspective.)

I can personally attest to the value of exercising this kind of discipline over finances. Even though Jill and I have made some mistakes, our basic commitment over the years to hold to a tight budget, tithe, avoid debt, and save and invest whatever we could, got us through low-pay (sometimes no-pay) ministry, career changes, a period of unemployment, the failure of a business venture and the building of a new business.

So, regardless of your situation, hold to sound principles. Make the commitment today:

    – to tithe
    – to get out and stay out of debt

– to start a contingency fund

– to start saving, investing, and protecting what you have been given

– to adopt The Ten Percent Solution target allocation of ten percent, ten percent, ten percent, and seventy percent as your own objective.

Success here will do more to assure that you reach your objectives than just about anything else. So take this seriously and put it to the test. You will be glad you did.

Individual Exercise

If you did not already fill in the target allocation (Figure 10A) and basic living expense forms (Figure 10C), do so now. Each do your own, with no discussion or sharing.

• Write down what you believe are the ten most important and/or essential budget expenditures you will have over the next two years. Rank them in order, with #1 being most important.

• Choose one response.
  (a) I think The Ten Percent Solution target allocation is unrealistic.
  (b) I think it is okay, but not that important.
  (c) I think it is an excellent target and would like to use it in our budget planning.

Discussion

First share, with no comment or criticism, only asking clarifying questions if you don't understand something. After sharing, discuss the following.

• In which areas are your forms and lists most similar? Most different?

• How close are you to The Ten Percent Solution target allocation goal?

• If it is not realistic for you now, can you visualize a point in the future at which you think you could reach this target and beyond? When would this be?

FIGURE 10B
Example of The 10% Solution
NEWLY-WEDS WITH $25,000 ANNUAL INCOME

10% TITHE	10% SAVINGS, INVESTMENT & LIFE INSURANCE	10% CONTINGENCY	70% LIVING EXPENSE
$2,500	$2,500	$2,500	$17,500

YOUR LIVING EXPENSE BUDGET

	ANNUAL	MONTHLY
Income (Fed., State & Local) & Soc. Sec. Taxes . $	3,000	250
Mortgage & Real Estate Taxes (or Rent) . . . . . . $	5,100	425
Food & Household . . . . $	3,000	250
Gas & Electric . . . . $	600	50
Other Utilities (Phone, water & sewer) . . . . $	900	75
Auto Payments . . . . $	1,344	112
Auto Escrow (For maintenance & repair) . . . . . $	600	50
Parking & Other Transportation . . . . $	180	15
Disability Insurance . . . . $	264	22
Auto & Home Insurance . . . . $	720	60
Clothing . . . . $	648	54
Recreation & Personal Gifts . . . . $	600	50
Vacation . . . . $	540	45
_____ . . . . $		
_____ . . . . $		
_____ . . . . $		
Misc. . . . . $	600	50
Budget Objective . . . . $	17,496	1,458

FIGURE 10C
The 10% Solution
Your Ideal Budget Schematic

10% TITHE	10% SAVINGS, INVESTMENT & LIFE INSURANCE	10% CONTINGENCY	70% LIVING EXPENSE

YOUR LIVING EXPENSE BUDGET

	ANNUAL	MONTHLY
Income (Fed., State & Local) & Soc. Sec. Taxes . $		
Mortgage & Real Estate Taxes (or Rent) . . . . . . $		
Food & Household . . . . $		
Gas & Electric . . . . $		
Other Utilities (Phone, water & sewer) . . . . $		
Auto Payments . . . . $		
Auto Escrow (For maintenance & repair) . . . . . $		
Parking & Other Transportation . . . . $		
Disability Insurance . . . . $		
Auto & Home Insurance . . . . $		
Clothing . . . . $		
Recreation & Personal Gifts . . . . $		
Vacation . . . . $		
_____ . . . . $		
_____ . . . . $		
_____ . . . . $		
Misc. . . . . $		
Budget Objective . . . . $		

FIGURE 10C
The 10% Solution
Your Ideal Budget Schematic

10% TITHE	10% SAVINGS, INVESTMENT & LIFE INSURANCE	10% CONTINGENCY	70% LIVING EXPENSE

YOUR LIVING EXPENSE BUDGET

	ANNUAL	MONTHLY
Income (Fed., State & Local) & Soc. Sec. Taxes . $		
Mortgage & Real Estate Taxes (or Rent) ...... $		
Food & Household .... $		
Gas & Electric .... $		
Other Utilities (Phone, water & sewer) .... $		
Auto Payments .... $		
Auto Escrow (For maintenance & repair) ..... $		
Parking & Other Transportation .... $		
Disability Insurance .... $		
Auto & Home Insurance .... $		
Clothing .... $		
Recreation & Personal Gifts .... $		
Vacation .... $		
_____ .... $		
_____ .... $		
_____ .... $		
Misc. .... $		
Budget Objective .... $		

ELEVEN

Dare to Dream

"Where there is no vision, the people perish."
(Proverbs 29:18, KJV)

The word translated as "vision" is translated elsewhere as "prophecy." Many people have a rather limited understanding of what prophecy is. When we hear the word, we tend to think of it in terms of predicting the future.

While the biblical prophets certainly did, from time to time, receive supernatural knowledge of the future, such special predictive powers were not an everyday occurrence. The prophets actually were more concerned with calling the people to remember the past, relate it to what was happening in the present, and on that basis make pronouncements regarding the future.

Interestingly, much of the prophecy about the future was articulated in an "if, then" manner. *If* the people responded and acted in one way, *then* God would bless them. In other words, the future was not completely preordained; there was more than one possible outcome, and the prophets often did nothing more than to describe the future effect of present attitudes and actions.

There are really two types of prophecy or vision: that which is specially given by God to an appointed prophet (what we call supernatural), and that which has to do with the understanding of history and the conditions of the present and their meaning for the future.

The visions and dreams I am encouraging you to

consider here are not of the supernatural variety. I am concerned here with the aspect of vision which involves the ability to imagine and conceptualize possibilities, both good and bad, for the future, to dream of the good and right things and order the present in such a way as to bring those dreams into being.

I want to encourage you to have a vision for your life and your finances. I am convinced that God wants us to dream, to imagine what we might be and do for Him.

Can you imagine what it would be like to be debt free? Is there a special place you would like to live? Would you like to take an extraordinary trip? Could you see yourself starting your own business? Would you like to give more of your time, money, and talent to ministry?

Go ahead! Dream on, asking God to show you which dreams He would like you to pursue. When your heart is seeking after His will and you are willing to apply yourself to the goal, then He just may "give you the desires of your heart." (See Psalm 37:4, also Psalm 37:3, Psalm 145:19, Proverbs 10:24, and Psalm 112:1 and following, especially verse 10 for balance.)

In financial planning, our dreams are expressed as goals or objectives. Without clearly defined objectives, it is difficult to plan. Therefore, a good plan begins with defining the objectives.

1. *Talk about your dreams and goals.*

What would you like to accomplish financially? You may have already talked with each other about some of your goals, such as buying a car or house. But chances are you have not discussed a lot of your goals in much detail, such as exactly when will the goal be reached, how much will it cost, and how you will pay for it.

Talking about these is important to your relationship. Many couples have never spoken about their dreams, and years later they harbor frustration and bitterness that might have been prevented if they had just talked early in the marriage. Do not assume your partner automatically understands you or your needs.

2. *Write them down.*

Take a few minutes right now to write down as many of your financial objectives as you can think of. Do it alone, first. Then come back together and share what you have written. Organize your page similarly to the following example, allowing some space for quantifying the objectives in terms of future costs as well as space for notes.

FIGURE 11A
Financial Objectives

Name of Objective	Define Specifically	Target Date	Estimated Cost	Comments
HOUSING	DOWNPAYMENT POINTS, EXP.	1992	15,000	70,000 HOUSE 15% DOWN
CAR(S)	MID-SIZED OLDS, USED	1991	8,000	
CAREER CHANGE/ ADVANCEMENT				
TRAVEL	VACATION	EACH SUMMER	600-800	
MINISTRY	1 MO. MISSION-MEX.	1993	2,000	
CHILDREN	1ST CHILD	1994	5,000	
FINANCIAL INDEPENDENCE	30,000/yr.	2015	400,000	INCOME FROM INVESTMENTS, HOUSE PAID FOR
GIVING	TITHE	1991	2,500/yr.	
EDUCATION				
AVOCATIONS/ HOBBIES				
PAY OFF DEBTS	AUTO, CREDIT CARDS	1991	200/mo.	

3. *Prioritize your objectives.*

Once you have made your initial list, assign items levels of priority. You can use the approach outlined in Chapter 5 or you can do a simplified version, such as Class A—High Priority, Class B—Medium Priority, and Class C—Low Priority. The method is not important as long as you are able to successfully prioritize your objectives.

4. *Quantify them.*

Put a price tag on your objectives. Some will be easy, some not so easy. For instance, a house is not too difficult. You can merely look at the real estate advertisements to get a rough idea of house prices in a geographic area. On the other hand, knowing what a career change will cost may require some more time-consuming research.

If your objective is more than a couple of years away, it is advisable to consider inflation. If a car costs $10,000 today, the price of a car increases at a five-percent annual rate, and you don't plan on buying the car until three years from now, your goal would be $11,576.

Give God Veto Power

Since stewardship is such an important concept in the Bible, it stands to reason that God would have us consider our planning and spending decisions carefully and prayerfully. Ask God to confirm that your decisions are the best they can be. When you desire something, give God "veto" power. This can be done in a number of ways.

The first is to ask God to change your desires if it is not right for you. Especially, ask Him for wisdom so that you are not fooled by your own feelings, ignorance, or hidden greed.

The second is to give God permission to change circumstances. As a last test, Jill and I sometimes will walk away from a purchase and come back later. If it is still there, and we have received no other understanding that dissuades us from that particular use of our resources, we will go ahead with it. If we can't walk away because we are afraid it won't be there later, that is a good indication that we are not trusting in our Provider as we should. This is also a good way to avoid being duped by high pressure salespeople who insist that they "can only hold this price for today." The vast majority of the time, such a pitch is simply not true.

A third way is to offer God a sort of financial "fleece." Sometimes it is really difficult to know what God's will is. By giving Him the purse strings, you can sometimes hear Him a bit better.

Jill and I left a full-time ministry because of such a

"fleece." Not certain whether we had completed our work, we decided to let God lead us through His provision. First, we set a reasonable target for the funding of the ministry. Then we let God know that if He did not want us to stay where we were, we did not want to make that fund-raising goal. If we were to stay, we would trust Him to supply.

When we told our staff and supporters this, we got a variety of reactions, mostly of puzzlement. Some thought it silly and others, I am sure, did not think we were serious. What was great is that God made it emphatic. Not only did we not reach the goal, we weren't even close. To many, I am sure that our fund drive appeared a dismal failure. To us it was a resounding success, and we were able to leave in great peace, confident that we were doing the right thing.

In other matters, we have implemented financial decisions because God did provide. I marvel at the rationalization processes many Christians employ to justify financial commitments, especially when it involves debt. Leaders of churches and organizations are masters of this. They see a need, design a program, hire people, and then worry about raising money. "We're stepping out on faith," they explain with great piety, and that shuts up most doubters.

But what is the greater demonstration of faith? Is it to commit and spend before God has provided, presuming upon His kindness to bail us out, or to pray and wait on Him to provide, only moving ahead as He verifies our desires and decisions with His provision? If God is big enough to bail us out when we irresponsibly go into debt, is He not big enough to provide up front?

Now I am not saying that we should never commit to any expense before full provision has occurred. Such an extreme carries its own fallacies. An organization or business often must make budgets and commit to expenditures in anticipation of provision. So must individuals. After all, Moses did not lead the people into the wilderness with everything in the bank, and Jesus did not require a full checking account before sending His disciples out to minister.

What I am saying is that we should be very careful not

to justify our own greed, ambition, or irresponsibility by using the "faith" argument. Rather, we should consider every way to offer God "veto power" over our financial objectives and decisions.

Dare to dream, but wait for confirmation of His provision.

TWELVE

Risk Management

I n 1984 Jill took our three children to see their grandparents. As they were returning home on the interstate, a large truck improperly changed lanes, hitting our car in the rear quarter panel. The high speed impact caused the car to swerve out of control, cross the lane, hit an embankment, and roll, finally ending up on its side.

When I got there some seven hours later and inspected what was left of our car, I was shocked to see that it was virtually destroyed; all that was left intact was the passenger cage, and even that was bent and crumpled. It was a miracle that, apart from some bruises on the kids, a sore neck and back for Jill, and psychological trauma that would heal with time and care, no one was seriously injured. Those who had seen the car right after the accident repetitively expressed amazement that no one was killed.

As I have told many people since, I believe in guardian angels, seat belts, and Oldsmobiles. Reflecting more extensively on why my family survived such an accident, I point to a number of key factors. A few seemingly small actions made the difference between life and death.

First, when we bought our car, we prayed about which one to choose. Although we knew that the Oldsmobile Cutlass was a sturdy midsized automobile, and safety was a consideration, we only found out later that it had one of the best crash ratings of all cars. Somehow, God's grace allowed us unconsciously to purchase the right car.

Second, Jill always made sure that she and the children were securely restrained in car seats and seat belts. When I think of what would have happened to my children, being hurled around inside that car, if they had not been restrained, I cannot understand how any parents who love their children can allow them to ride without safety restraints.

Providence, foresight, and planning made the difference. Had we not purchased that particular automobile, and had Jill not been diligent in her responsibility, who knows what tragedy might have occurred?

One other aspect of our planning was of great assistance in the aftermath; we were adequately insured. Though we suffered some financial loss, it was minimal compared to what it could have been.

Life is full of risks. Every day we find ourselves in a world that presents threats to our property, our health, and our lives. Risk management is a term describing the acknowledgment, assessment, and preparation involved in reducing risk as well as providing means with which to carry on when risk becomes reality.

Jill acknowledged the risk of an accident. To reduce that risk and the damage it could do, she drove carefully and made sure everyone used seat belts. But even such care cannot always keep an accident from occurring. Savings and insurance provided enough money to avoid severe financial crisis when the risk of accident became the reality of a "totaled" automobile.

If you want to exercise good risk management, avoid the two extreme errors that many of us make at one time or another.

The Ostrich Head Fake

The ostrich head fake is a paranoid reaction to both known and unknown risks. Fear dominates, producing an unhealthy conservatism. Focusing on the risk results in the inability to venture. Preferring to hide out and avoid dealing with the risk, procrastination, ignorance, and preservation of status quo become the primary activities. Not only will the ostrich head fake result in many lost opportunities, it may even expose us to additional risks. It is a prescription for financial failure.

Hiding is not living. If a parent tries to risk-proof a child, that poor youth would end up in a padded room and never be allowed to venture outside, just because "something bad might happen." Perhaps you recall the man referred to by Amos who encounters a lion, runs in fear and escapes, then meets a bear, and again runs in fear only to arrive safely at home, where he relaxes, leans against the wall, and is bitten by a serpent (Amos 5:19). I am taking this passage out of context, but its irony still has some application to the fact that, sometimes, in our fearful desire to escape risks, we may encounter something just as risky or worse.

Christians are not to live a life of fear. Paul wrote that "God did not give us a spirit of timidity but a spirit of power and love and self-control" (II Timothy 1:7). Many times the Lord began a message to His people with the words, "Fear not."

The Daredevil Plunge

The other extreme is a negligent ignoring of risk with what often would be described as a complete lack of common sense. The thinking of such venturing is marked by such thoughts as "It won't happen to me" and "I feel lucky today." It is also noted for impulsive behavior and decision making.

The focus is on personal convenience, pleasure, and gain. Seat belts are inconvenient and confining, so I won't wear one. I know I can't afford that car, and I'm already in too much debt, but it's what I've always wanted—if I get a longer loan, I should be able to make the payments. I know I should keep this money for emergencies, but with this deal I stand to triple my money within five years!

Just as fear can destroy, so can recklessness and impulsiveness. While we are to be bold, we are also to be prudent. Consider the wisdom of the Book of Proverbs: "The plans of the diligent lead surely to abundance, but every one who is hasty comes only to want" (21:5). "The simple believes everything, but the prudent looks where he is going" (14:15).

We should not be paranoid regarding risks. Neither should we ignore risks with either unfounded optimism or blind fatalism. Rather, we should be intelligently aware of our risks, measure them as accurately as possible, and manage our affairs so as to minimize those risks while still moving steadily ahead.

Identify Your Risks

Jill knew that driving an automobile entailed the risk of a wreck. Though accidents had always happened to "someone else," she was not so foolish as to think it couldn't happen to her. Nor was she going to refuse to drive just because it is possible to crash. Realistically identifying a collision as one of her risks was essential if she was going to be able to do anything about minimizing that risk.

Similarly, financial risks need to be correctly and realistically identified and considered whenever you make financial decisions. Risks are enemies to your financial health, and as the old adage instructs, "Know thine enemy."

Among the more common financial risks which should be considered in your financial risk management are the following:

Job or income loss—One can be laid off or fired or choose to leave a job or profession, any of which can cause an interruption of income.

Health problems—Health conditions can affect both our ability to make money and how we spend it.

Disability—Due to physical illness or accident or mental illness, we may become disabled and prevented from earning an income or from earning the type of income to which we are accustomed.

Death—While our death may have no financial significance to ourselves, it has tremendous financial significance for those who depend on us. And the death of family and others with whom we have financial interdependence (such as a business partner) can have a devastating effect on us.

Investment risk—Investments can go sour. Companies can go bankrupt, property can be damaged, and people can defraud. Regardless of what the market does, each investment will attain its own level of success or failure.

Market risk—Any investment can be affected by the market it is in. If the market moves one way or another, it may tend to pull the particular investment with it.

Interest rate risk—If you lock in a CD or bond for five years, you run the risk that rates will go up, thereby depriving you of the higher rate or forcing you to take a penalty or loss for liquidating it before maturity.

Inflation risk—If you lock in income, as inflation progresses, your purchasing power decreases. In other words, if inflation averages seven and two-tenths percent, a hundred dollars will only buy fifty dollars worth of groceries ten years from now.

Deflation risk—If you buy a home for $60,000, putting $6,000 down and the economy goes into a deflationary cycle which lowers the cost of everything twenty percent, you will owe more than your house is worth.

Depreciation risk—The value of most consumer goods, including automobiles, clothing, and computers, decreases dramatically as soon as you take possession. Should you get in financial trouble the following month and try to sell such items, you will most likely lose money. This loss will be magnified to the extent you borrowed to make the purchase.

Consider the Worst Case Scenario

Before making a significant financial decision, identify the type(s) of risks involved. Then ask yourself, "What is the worst thing that can happen if I proceed with this?" The simplest and most accurate way to answer this question is to ask a series of "what if" questions.

- What if I lose my job/income through layoff, disability, business failure, or investment failure?
- What if I have major health problems?
- What if I die?

These questions should be asked when you are considering the purchase of a home, automobile, or investment. They should especially be asked anytime you consider making a financial commitment that involves debt financing.

If you start your own business or become part owner of a business from which you also earn your income, these questions should be asked and answered every year, along with some other questions.

- What if the business has a bad year and my expected income is cut by one third or one half?
- What kind of conditions would cause this business to suffer or even fail? Are such conditions at all likely in the next few years?
- If you have a partner or partners, what would happen if they were disabled or killed?

Such questions should be discussed with your attorney, accountant, and other financial advisers.

When considering an investment, add these questions:

- Will I need this money anytime in the near future?
- What is the volatility of the market and type of investment involved? (Can the market this investment is in drop or rise precipitously in a short period of time, and what would happen to this investment if it did?)
- If there is investment risk, what would happen if the company's earnings dropped significantly or if it went bankrupt? (What if management made some serious mistakes or its major product was tampered with?)
- What would happen if I need to liquidate this investment in the event of an emergency? What is the likelihood of any of this occurring?

Once you have honestly and accurately identified the worst case, you can now consider whether the probability of success justifies the risk involved.

Plan for Investment and Market Risk

A financial plan that properly considers risk will anticipate such risks and provide contingency plans if things go wrong. Such protection often comes under the headings of insurance and/or hedges.

For instance, a person who buys real estate protects his family by purchasing some life insurance to cover indebtedness and the fact that real estate may not be very liquid at the time his family would need the money. Or a person sets aside cash in a savings account equal to six months of bills in case he loses his job or some other difficulty befalls him. This is *insurance.*

If a person buys stocks he might also buy some gold or an investment in some other market that may go up if the stock market goes down. This is called *hedging.*

One of the most basic and reliable methods of reducing risk is *diversification.* The old adage about not putting all your eggs in one basket is common sense, yet I am amazed to see how many people ignore this time-tested bit of sagacity. If you own one stock, and the company goes bankrupt, you could lose all of your money. But if you own twenty stocks, what is the probability that all twenty companies will go under?

Similarly, if you only own stocks, and the market drops twenty percent, the probability is that you will lose a similar percentage of value. But if you own stocks and also own CDs and an equipment-leasing partnership, your total portfolio might sustain only a small percentage loss or no loss at all.

Insurance and Self-Insurance Concepts

Insurance is the premier risk-management tool. Simply defined, insurance is an amount of assets set aside to be available in case something bad happens. The story of Joseph in Egypt (Genesis 41:25-57) shows the idea of insurance working in dramatic fashion. Joseph made the people pay "premiums" into a central storehouse during the good times, so that they could draw on that storehouse during the bad times that he knew were coming.

There are two basic kinds of insurance, self-provided and that which is provided by an outside entity (i.e., an insurance company). Self-insurance means that the person or entity with the risk sets aside money in the budget or in an actual account for that risk. An insurance company collects and invests premiums from many individuals and/or entities and provides a pool of funds from which a policy owner may draw if covered losses are sustained. It is a practical way for the many who are blessed with no losses to help provide for those who suffer loss.

Insurance and self-insurance concepts are often combined. An example is health insurance with a deductible and coinsurance provisions. You cover yourself via savings and budget for the deductible and coinsurance amounts, while the insurance company covers you for any additional amounts.

But Shouldn't We Trust in God to Take Care of Us?

Occasionally, I hear a Christian object to insurance (or savings, investments, or other aspects of planning) with the "faith" argument. If you have used such an argument to avoid prudent planning, consider again the lesson of Joseph. And what do you think Paul was talking about when he instructed Timothy, "If any one does not provide for his relatives, and especially for his own family, he has disowned the faith and is worse than an unbeliever" (I Timothy 5:8)? What does this say about someone who dies and leaves the family with debts and obligations and no assets with which to provide for them?

When you drive your car, should you ignore seat belts, fail to service the brakes, and go without insurance because you have faith that God will keep you safe? That's not faith; that's stupidity.

What to Insure and How to Insure It

Figure 12A, found at the end of this chapter, lists the areas of life to be insured that are common to married couples. Also included is a brief description of how to insure each. "Policy" refers to a policy or policies issued by an insurance company. "SI" (Self-Insurance) refers to a savings or investment account to be drawn upon if needed. Also included are some thoughts about when to insure and when to review your needs to update and verify that you are sufficiently covered. An "*" indicates a top priority that should be taken care of immediately; do not procrastinate.

Buying insurance can be a confusing and intimidating process. Sales hype, computerized projections, magazine articles, and claims and counterclaims regarding what is best all combine in a barrage of information that can reduce any reasonable being to a frustrated and fatalistic surrender.

Between ten and fifteen percent of a typical household budget goes to insurance premiums of one sort or another. The good news is that there are ways to make the process of purchasing insurance easier and less costly.

Some Tips on Buying Insurance

1. *First, choose a qualified and experienced financial consultant/planner or insurance agent to help you.*

Interview two or three about their methods and philosophy of insurance planning. Let them know up front that you are not there this time to buy insurance, but to find out how they do business and what their qualifications are. This puts the initial meeting in a more relaxed atmosphere, puts product sales in the background, and allows you to explore and get to know each other a little.

Some things to look for:

- A good reputation—recommendations from satisfied clients.
- A compatible personality and values—some people just don't function well with certain personality types. If

the agent is a Christian, so much the better, if he or she is also competent.

– Genuine concern for you and your needs.
– Credentials—Look for professional designations such as ChFC (Chartered Financial Consultant) and CFP (Certified Financial Planner) for those who practice broader financial consulting/planning and CLU (Chartered Life Underwriter) for those who emphasize insurance primarily. Also look for membership in industry and professional associations such as the International Association of Financial Planners, the National Association of Life Underwriters and the American Society of CLU and ChFC.
– Knowledge—Rather than shopping for policies, first shop for brains. If you find a good agent, stick with him or her, because your agent's knowledge will probably be more valuable in the long run than saving a few dollars in premiums in the short run.

A professional insurance agent should demonstrate a thorough knowledge of insurance products and the laws and situations that affect their usage, be able to inform you of alternatives and help you understand the advantages and disadvantages of each so you can make intelligent decisions, and be involved in ongoing industry education programs.

– Good backup and services capability—A professional insurance agent should have associates, technical experts, and service personnel available, if not in-house, then through formal or informal associations with companies and organizations.
– Strong company affiliations—Some agents sell only with one insurance company. This is fine, as long as that company is financially strong and they have a good version of the product you need. Other agents will have a "primary" company or companies, but are able to go to other companies to find the product that best meets your needs.

If you find a good agent who works with many companies, it is often helpful if the agent can "shop the market" for you. Agents will tend to look out for your best interests and work harder for you if you are loyal to them. You will save time and avoid the hassle and confusion inherent in multiple agent competition where everyone is making claims and counterclaims about their products and why they are better than the next guy's. Generally, larger companies will be able to weather financial hazards better than small companies. I like to look for companies with a billion or more dollars of assets and a rating of A + (Superior) by the A. M. Best Company. Occasionally I will use smaller companies for a particular situation, but only after I am satisfied that they are financially sound and run in a manner likely to keep them so.

2. Beware of those who say there is only one way (their way, of course) to do things.

For instance, you may run across a salesperson who says that you should "never buy a cash-value life insurance policy," asserting that you should only buy term insurance. The fact is that cash-value life insurance is often the best solution. My own analyses have confirmed over and over again that if I want to keep my life insurance for ten years or more, there is a reasonable probability that universal life or whole life will be more cost-effective for me. Using reasonable investment assumptions and considering the tax advantages of cash-value policies, I have seen break-even points of less than ten years.

3. Buy life, health, and disability insurance while you can.

With the specter of huge AIDS claims liability in the future, insurers have been tightening underwriting requirements and are currently instituting premium increases even for such insurance as life and disability, which had been decreasing over the past couple decades. Also, if you develop a health problem, such as high blood pressure or diabetes, you may have to pay extra, or may even find yourself unable to obtain coverage.

When buying insurance, try to anticipate future needs. Add riders guaranteeing future insurability if they are offered. Buy disability policies that are noncancelable and guaranteed renewable at the original rates. Buy health insurance that cannot be canceled. Understand that most life insurance policies are sold at current rates and values, but have guaranteed rates which describe the worst case scenario. Make sure your agent discusses these parameters and that you don't underfund the policy. With universal life policies, the more money you put in up front, the more secure your future ability to afford insurance will be. If you buy term, you should be saving aggressively in a side fund to cover future higher premiums.

4. *Never give up a policy unless you*

- are absolutely sure you don't need it now and won't need it in the future or
- a new, better policy is approved and "in force."

Replacement is often better for the agent than it is for you. Be sure that the agent and you have done your homework and are sure that replacement is in your best interest.

5. *Beware of mail-order insurance that requires little proof of insurability even though it advertises it "at group rates."*

"Group" is not synonymous with "inexpensive." It all depends on the group. If the group is full of cancer patients, the group rates are going to be high. I have almost never seen mail-order group rates that I have not been able to get cheaper with an individual policy if the person is healthy. This is true of most bank mortgage and credit insurance, too. If you are healthy you will probably be able to buy coverage through your agent for much less.

6. *Avoid mortgage and credit life insurance.*

Banks are notorious for automatically including mortgage or credit life insurance and either not calling it to your attention or presenting it in such a way as to make you think there is no alternative. They may even use intimidating practices to make you buy it even if you question it. Generally, these insurance coverages are overly expensive, just like the mail-order "group" policies. It is better if you build this kind of protection into your regular life and disability policies, which, if you are healthy, you will be able to obtain for much less. If the bank tells you it is required, question it and check your state laws; it may be illegal to make the granting of a consumer loan contingent on your agreement to buy the insurance. At worst, you should have the right to buy your own policy and make the bank a beneficiary up to the loan balance.

7. *When determining the amount of insurance you want, ask your agent to help you determine three levels of protection— minimal, comfortable, and ideal.*

Good, knowledgeable agents will follow a sound, scientific formula to help you determine how much protection you need and want. If they don't have and offer to use such a formula, you might want to consult another agent. Avoid an agent who says you should have such and such an amount because everyone your age should, or for any other reason you cannot understand and agree with. Every person's situation is different and insurance should be adapted to that particular situation. There is no one solution that neatly fits everyone.

8. *Whenever possible, try to factor inflation into your calculations, along with other future considerations, such as family, career, and income changes.*

Good planning includes an attempt to forecast the future under best case/worst case scenarios.

When buying property and casualty insurance (homeowners', auto, etc.), make sure any property is insured for its "replacement value." This is very important. Because of inflation, property tends to cost more to replace than it did to buy originally. Also, property tends to depreciate over time. Therefore, insuring for the purchase price or actual cash value is insufficient.

Also, if you have antiques or other items of unusual value, you may want to insure them separately. Replacement value in a regular policy only refers to a normal range of cost. Keeping a photo inventory and getting professional appraisals of valuable property is the best way of verifying claims. And put these in a safe-deposit box at your bank; they will do you no good if they are lost in a fire along with everything else.

Avoid buying insurance for narrowly defined benefits such as life insurance for airline flights and small items such as telephone lines or extended product warranties.

Some insurance policies that probably should be avoided: Collision insurance on rental cars (have this protection included in your personal auto policy for a fraction of the cost). Cancer insurance (it's expensive and should be covered under your major medical anyway). Accidental death insurance (if you have enough insurance if you die of a disease, you have enough—it's better to be adequately insured for death by any cause). Pet health insurance (premiums are high enough to make it unlikely to really benefit you unless the pet is chronically ill). Contact lens insurance (unless you are constantly losing lenses, it will probably be cheaper to self-insure).

In most cases, it is better to self-insure these with savings or include them in larger policies. Like most anything else, insurance is more cost-effective when it can be bought in large amounts, and it is expensive when bought in small amounts.

Few people like paying insurance premiums. Insurance is one of those necessities that people love to hate. It's not something you enjoy watching or playing with. It doesn't taste good and it won't provide hours of mad fun. But don't let negative feelings prevent you from being wise and responsible.

FIGURE 12A
Insurance

What to Insure	How to Insure	When to Insure	When to Review
* Hospitalization & Health Care	SI for deductibles & Co-ins., POLICY for catastrophic for at least $1 million	Immediately	Every 2 years or when life situation changes
* Disability (Sickness or accident, for 50%-70% of gross income)	SI for 3-6 mos., POLICY for min. of 5 yrs, ideally to age 65 or for life (cover for both total & partial disability if possible)	Immediately	Whenever your income, job, or group insurance changes
Loss of Life	SI & POLICIES to pay for funeral, debts, income replacement, taxes, liquidity	As soon as possible or when analysis shows need	Every 2-3 years or when changes in life of finances occur (kids, etc.)
* Auto Liability	POLICY	Immediately	Every 1-2 years
Auto Collision	SI for deductible, POLICY for balance of value	As soon as possible	Every 1-2 years
Auto Maint. & Repair	SI = to 5-10% of new car cost & 20-30% of value for cars older than 3 yrs. or 50,000 mi.	As soon as possible	Every year
* Homeowners, or Renters (Fire, theft, and other damage)	SI for deductible, POLICY for replace value of structure and contents	Immediately	Every 2-3 years
* General Liability	POLICY for misc. Damages occurring on your property or caused by you or family members	Immediately	Every 2-3 years

Exercise

• Referring to Figure 12A, which areas do you presently have taken care of, either with an insurance policy or with savings?

• In which areas are you underinsured?

• Which areas are you not sure about?

Discussion

Discuss the above questions and decide which areas need attention. If they require the assistance of a financial consultant/planner and/or insurance agent, discuss who and when, and call to make an appointment today.

THIRTEEN

Make a Basic Plan

Plans are made to be changed, but you can't change something that doesn't exist.

If you have completed your net worth statement, filled out your budget work sheets, defined your objectives, and identified your risks, then you are ready to make a written plan. Before doing this, however, I want to call your attention to two important elements essential to creating plans that will work.

Make Realistic Assumptions

Assumptions are the variables on which your plans are based. They can include investment rates of return, inflation rates, amounts of cash flow utilized, tax rates, and time available. If your assumptions are bad, you will be likely to produce an unrealistic and distorted plan.

For instance, you probably do not want to use a twelve percent projected rate of return if you plan to be investing in conservative instruments such as bank certificates of deposit (CDs). If the going rate for those CDs is currently eight and a half percent and long-term averages (ten years or longer) are below ten percent, that would be overly optimistic.

Likewise, a twenty-percent projected annual return would be too high for a stock mutual fund. Over the last sixty years, the S&P 500 with dividends and capital gains reinvested made an equivalent annualized return of just less than ten percent. Only the best ten-year periods returned more than twenty percent, and that is recent history. It would be much more realistic to assume a ten- to twelve-percent return on a growth stock fund.

Assumptions for a given investment should have at least a reasonably accurate historical relationship to other investments and inflation. Figure 13A offers some reasonable rates of return for investments against an assumed inflation rate between four percent and five percent and time periods of ten to twenty years. Current economic conditions could call for slightly higher or lower assumptions. For instance, if interest rates are high and can be locked in for the time period involved, then a higher assumption could be justified.

FIGURE 13A

Planning Assumptions for Selected Investments

(Believable total return in light of long-term historical performance data)

Inflation	4.0 - 5.0%
T-bills, money markets	4.5 - 6.0%
1-3 year CDs, treasury bonds	5.0 - 6.7%
Corporate bond funds (2-5 year mat.)	6.0 - 7.5%
Long-term treasuries, CDs	6.5 - 8.5%
Growth stock funds	9.0 - 12.0%
Aggressive growth stock funds	10.0 - 14.0%
Investment real estate	6.5 - 14.0%

Allocate Cash Flow and Assets Wisely

Allocation is the process by which you decide where to put your money and property and in what amounts. Your budget plan allocates your cash flow, while your investment plan allocates accumulated assets and cash flow budgeted for investments.

Wise allocation diversifies investments and property into categories consistent with your objectives, risk tolerance, and market conditions.

For instance, if you are allocating some money to buy a car in two years, it would not be appropriate to put those funds into a limited partnership that would tie the capital up for at least five to seven years. Not only would the money not be available in two years, there would probably be much more risk involved, which is not appropriate for short-term, conservative objectives. A five-year CD would not be appropriate either; even though a CD is safe, you would pay a penalty to withdraw it in two years. And while stocks are liquid, the risk would be a concern. A one- to two-year CD would probably be the most appropriate choice.

It is important to remember that investments should be targeted to specific objectives. Automobiles, house down payments, college educations, starting a business, and retirement are all specific objectives which should be considered separately for allocation purposes. (See Figure 13B.)

FIGURE 13B
Allocation Examples

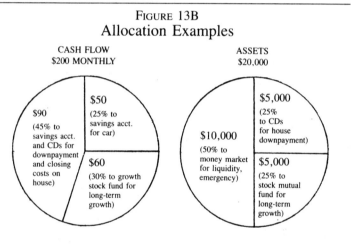

How Much Insurance Do You Need?

Most newlyweds need certain basic insurance plans. Use the following guides to decide what you need in each category. What follows is a sort of do-it-yourself guide. If you find exercises like this difficult, now is the time to find a professional to help you. If you enjoy this kind of work, do as much as you can and then have a professional look it over and offer recommendations.

HEALTH INSURANCE
(Consult employee benefit booklets, plan administrators, insurance agents, and/or planners if you need help.)

	YOU	SPOUSE
Do you have an employer-provided plan?	_____	_____
Or do you own your own health policy?	_____	_____
What is the maximum benefit?	_____	_____
What is the deductible?	_____	_____
What is the coinsurance arrangment?	_____	_____
What is the maximum out-of-pocket expense you could incur in a calendar year?	_____	_____
If you both have policies, is there duplicate coverage that could be waived?	_____	_____

DISABILITY INSURANCE

	YOU	SPOUSE
If you were disabled and could not work, how much after-tax monthly income would you need to replace to live reasonably? (A)	_____	_____
How much short-term disability insurance (monthly) do you have to cover the first six months of disability? (B)	_____	_____
How much do you have in emergency funds, divided by six? (Example: $6,000/6 = $1000 per month) (C)	_____	_____

Subtract B and C from A. If B + C is less than A, then you may want to put more into your emergency account or add short-term insurance.

Short-term (first six months) disability income need	_____	_____
How much group long-term disability insurance do you have (monthly benefit)? (D)	_____	_____
How long will it last?	_____	_____
How much personally owned disability insurance do you have (monthly benefit)? (E)	_____	_____
How long will it last?	_____	_____

How much monthly income could you get from
investments without invading the investment
principal? (F)   _____   _____

Subtract D, E, and F from A. If D + E + F is less than A, than the
difference is the amount of additional insurance needed.

Long-term disability income need   _____   _____

     Some additional considerations regarding disability insurance
should be discussed. Are there any coverages that do not last till age sixty-
five or longer? Should they? Does the insurance only cover you for total
disability, or is there a benefit for partial disability? Do you have to be
totally disabled before you can receive partial disability benefits? Does your
insurance cover your own occupation, any reasonable occupation, or does
it require you to be a vegetable to receive anything? As you can see, the
answers to these questions can greatly affect your need for insurance.

LIFE INSURANCE

This is a very basic analysis. However, it would meet the requirements of
most newlyweds on a first marriage with no children.

If you died tomorrow . . .
FOR WHAT NEEDS WOULD YOU WANT TO PROVIDE?

	YOU	SPOUSE
How much would it cost in "final expenses" (funeral, probate, taxes, etc.)? If unknown, put $15,000-20,000.	_____	_____
Would you want to pay off your debts to give your spouse a "clean slate"? If so, add up the balances of all debts.	_____	_____
Would you want to provide some extra money to replace some income for your spouse? (Example: $50,000 would produce $5,000 per year indefinitely, or $6,000 per year for about fifteen years, at a ten-percent investment rate.)	_____	_____
Would you want to leave something for anyone else or as a charitable gift? (If you have children, own a business, or have other needs, include them here. For example, you might want to provide money for a child's college education.)	_____	_____

Total amount needed to meet need (A)
  (add the four numbers above) $_____ $ _____

WHAT ASSETS ARE CURRENTLY AVAILABLE TO MEET THE NEED CALCULATED ABOVE?

Group life insurance   _____   _____

Personally owned life insurance   _____   _____

Checking, money funds, savings accounts   _____   _____

CDs, savings bonds   _____   _____

Stocks, bonds, mutual funds   _____   _____

Death benefits from pensions, IRAs   _____   _____

Total amount available to meet need (B)
(add the seven numbers above)   _____   _____

Life insurance needed
Subtract B from A. If B is smaller than A, then the difference is the amount of new insurance needed.

$_____   \$ _____

AUTO INSURANCE

Are you fully covered for liability, including the other car and medical costs for its occupants? Are you covered for collision to your own car(s)? What is your deductible? If you totaled your car, how much would your policy pay, and would that be sufficient? Does your policy cover occasional drivers? Does it cover you when you rent a car, including collision on the rental car?

HOMEOWNERS' OR RENTERS' INSURANCE

Does your policy cover market value or replacement cost? (You want replacement cost.) Do you have any especially valuable antiques, jewelry, etc., that should be separately insured? What is the maximum protection under this policy, including any riders? Does your policy include umbrella liability in case someone is injured on your property or for other unusual occurrences?

Project the Future

To make good allocation decisions, it will help to take your objectives and make some trial projections at your assumed inflation and investment rates. Let's say you want to buy a house in five years. The approximate price of the house you hope to buy is $60,000 today, and you want to put down $10,000, including closing costs.

First, consider inflation. If we assume that inflation on homes will average four percent, the house will cost almost $73,000 in five years, and the down payment and closing costs will be over $12,000. Therefore, your target is at least $12,000. (It probably should be more, since there are always fix-up and moving costs associated with home ownership.)

Now, if you have $10,000 saved, and $6,000 is to be allocated for emergency, you would have $4,000 to allocate to the future house. If you invest the $4,000 in a five-year CD paying an annual yield of eight and a half percent, it would grow to $6,015 in five years.

Since that will not be enough to reach your $12,000 goal, you will need to allocate some cash flow from your budget to make up the approximately $6,000 projected shortage. Using an interest rate table, computer, or calculator, you can determine exactly how much you will have to save each month at a given rate of return to reach your goal. In this example, it would take approximately $80 per month saved at eight and a half percent to accumulate another $6,000 in five years.

Books with compound interest rate, sinking fund, and loan amortization tables can be found in most major bookstores and libraries. If you have a computer, there are also numerous home finance programs available for most personal computer models. A competent planner, insurance agent, stockbroker, or accountant will also be able to help you with these kinds of projections. In fact, I strongly recommend getting some professional help at this stage of your planning.

Figure 13D (at the end of this chapter) is a simple spread-sheet program I designed to model such projections for my clients. It shows such a projection, using three accounts and assumptions from the sample allocation plan shown in Figure 13C.

Example of Newlyweds' Basic Allocation Plan

ASSET ALLOCATION PLAN

	Existing Allocation	Proposed Allocation	Type of Financial Product
Cash/emergency	$14,000	$6,000	Money market, savings
For house	0	$4,000	2-5 year CD
For next car	0	$2,000	2 year CD
Escrow for repairs, clothing, misc.	0	$1,000	Savings
Long-term invest	0	$1,000	Growth stock Mutual fund

CASH FLOW ALLOCATION PLAN (monthly)

Life insurance	$15	$25	Ann. renewable term
Disability insurance	0	$30	Noncancelable, guar.
Escrow—insurance (home, auto)	0	$75	Savings
Escrow—repairs, clothing, etc.	0	$25	Savings, CDs
For house	$100	$80	Savings, CDs
For next car	0	$50	Savings, CDs
Long-term invest	0	$50	Mutual Fund
Contingency/misc.	$150	$25	Money market
Totals	*$265*	*$360*	

Such projections will help give you an idea of whether your goals and ability to reach those goals are realistic or not. If various allocation approaches show that your current allocated resources are insufficient to reach your goals, you may need to change your goals and/or your allocation.

As you can see, the new allocation requires $95 more per month than what they were used to saving. But they were paying for clothes, repairs, etc., out of cash flow anyway, so this is really not as much of an increase as it might appear.

The results of the proposed allocation shown in Figure 13C would be as follows:

In five years, they would have over $12,500 available for a house.

In three years, approximately $5,000 would be available for a car.

In five years, the long-term investment account would have over $5,800 in it, and almost $14,000 in ten years.

The various escrow and contingency funds should have provided reasonably well for those purposes.

Now, this assumes that they do not receive an increase in income with which to increase their savings and investment contributions. If their income increases, they will be that much better off.

Who Will Pay the Bills? and Other Sticky Wickets

At this point, it is a good idea to discuss who will be responsible for handling the mechanics of the budget as well as taxes and investments. One of you may pay the monthly bills and make sure deposits are made to the various escrow and investment accounts. The other may take responsibility for food and supply purchases and auto servicing. You may decide to tackle tax records and forms together.

However, it is a good idea to switch responsibilities or at least participate with each other from time to time, so you both are up-to-date and reasonably knowledgeable about all of your financial affairs. This allocation of your talents and responsibilities is a very important part of your financial plan. If the practical mechanics are not working, then even the best plans can fail.

Individual Exercise

If you did not fill out the insurance need analyses, do so now.

- On separate sheets of paper, write out an allocation plan for your existing savings and investments and cash flow, using Figure 13C and Section VII of the form at the end of this chapter as a guide. (You can also refer back to the budget guides in Chapter 10.)

- Would you prefer to set up separate accounts for various purposes, or have just a few accounts and keep a separate ledger showing the purposes for the money?

• Who do you think should have primary responsibility for the following?

Category	You	Your Spouse	Both
Food shopping			
Paying bills			
Making savings & investments deposits			
Record keeping			
Tax forms and payments			
Auto service			
Other			

• Is this a good time to consult an insurance agent, investment broker, accountant and/or financial planner? If so, list the names of any you know.

Discussion

• Compare your basic insurance need analyses. Where are they similar? different?

• Compare your allocation plans. Where are they similar? Where do they differ? Can you compromise and make some decisions now?

• Compare your answers to the question about setting up different accounts. Note where they are similar and where they differ. What accounts (i.e., savings, money markets, insurance, investments) do you think you should open now?

• Compare your answers to who should be responsible for what. Circle those areas in which you agree. Discuss and try to decide on those areas in which you disagree.

• Discuss your responses to the need for professional help. If you agree it is time to see someone, whom do you want to call, and which of you will set the appointment?

• Write down your basic plan using the charts on pages 126-132 as a guideline. (Refer back to examples in this chapter and chapters 9 and 10.)

FIGURE 13D
Investment Account Projections

CLIENT: NEWLY-WED COUPLE, GROSS INCOME $25,000   DATE: 01/01/89

Investment Rates:
ACCT #1: 7.5% MONEY MKT, CDs
ACCT #2: 8.2% MONEY MKT, CD'S, GOV'T SECS, ETC.
ACCT #3: 11.0% STOCKS, BONDS, MUT. FUNDS, ETC.

Current Amounts Accumulated:
ACCT #1: $7,000
ACCT #2: $6,000
ACCT #3: $1,000

ACCT #1: CONTINGENCY, ESCROW

YEAR	PROJECTED ANNUAL AMOUNT INVESTED	PROJECTED ANNUAL WITHDRAWAL	PROJECTED ACCOUNT BALANCE @ 7.5%
1	$2,160	($1,900)	$7,805
2	$2,160	($1,845)	$8,728
3	$2,160	($1,950)	$9,609
4	$2,160	($1,965)	$10,539
5	$2,160	($2,854)	$10,584
6	$2,160	($3,059)	$10,411
7	$2,160	($4,900)	$8,246
8	$2,160	($2,075)	$8,956
9	$2,160	($2,150)	$9,638
10	$2,160	($2,490)	$10,007

ACCT #2: CAR, HOME PURCHASE

YEAR	PROJECTED ANNUAL AMOUNT INVESTED	PROJECTED ANNUAL WITHDRAWAL	PROJECTED ACCOUNT BALANCE @ 8.2%
1	$1,560	$0	$8,180
2	$1,560	$0	$10,539
3	$1,560	$0	$13,091
4	$1,560	($5,000)CAR	$10,442
5	$1,560	$0	$12,986
6	$1,560	($12,500)HOM	$2,214
7	$1,560	$0	$3,956
8	$1,560	$0	$5,840
9	$1,560	$0	$7,879
10	$1,560	$0	$10,085

ACCT #3: LONG-TERM INVESTMENTS

YEAR	PROJECTED ANNUAL AMOUNT INVESTED	PROJECTED ANNUAL WITHDRAWAL	PROJECTED ACCOUNT BALANCE @ 11.0%
1	$600	$0	$1,776
2	$600	$0	$2,637
3	$600	$0	$3,593
4	$600	$0	$4,655
5	$600	$0	$5,833
6	$600	$0	$7,140
7	$600	$0	$8,592
8	$600	$0	$10,203
9	$600	$0	$11,991
10	$600	$0	$13,976

SUMMARY OF COMBINED ACCOUNTS

YEAR	PROJECTED COMBINED ANNUAL AMOUNT INVESTED	PROJECTED COMBINED ANNUAL WITHDRAWAL	PROJECTED COMBINED ACCOUNT BALANCE
1	$4,320	($1,900)	$17,760
2	$4,320	($1,845)	$21,904
3	$4,320	($1,950)	$26,293
4	$4,320	($5,965)	$25,636
5	$4,320	($2,854)	$29,402
6	$4,320	($15,559)	$19,765
7	$4,320	($4,900)	$20,794
8	$4,320	($2,075)	$24,999
9	$4,320	($2,150)	$29,508
10	$4,320	($2,490)	$34,068

ALLOCATION FROM FIG. 13 C:

FOR CAR - $2,000 EXISTING PLUS $50 PER MONTH

FOR HOME PURCHASE - $4,000 EXISTING PLUS $80 PER MONTH

LONG TERM INVESTMENT - $1,000 EXISTING PLUS $50 PER MONTH

CONTINGENCY, ESCROW - $6,000 EXISTING PLUS $180 PER MONTH

SINCE ESCROW FOR BUDGETED ITEMS IS INCLUDED, DEPOSITS SHOWN
ARE MUCH LESS THAN 10% CONTINGENCY & SAVINGS/INVEST TARGETS

ACCOUNT BALANCES SHOWN AT END OF YEAR

WITHDRAWALS MADE BEGINNING OF YEAR

DEPOSITS MADE BEGINNING OF YEAR

DEPOSITS SHOWN ARE 17.3% OF $25,000 INCOME
(8.6% CONTINGENCY & ESCROW, 8.7% SAVINGS & INVESTMENT)

Our Basic Financial Plan
SECTION I
Personal Data

NAME: _____ DATE _____

ADDRESS: _____ CITY _____ STATE _____ ZIP _____

	YOU: _____	SPOUSE: _____
EMPLOYER		
EMPLOYER ADDRESS		
POSITION/ OCCUPATION DESCRIPTION		
ANN EARNED INCOME		
HEALTH CONDITIONS		
PARENTS NAMES/AGE		
BROTHERS/ SISTERS		

CHILDREN	NAMES	BIRTHDATES

IMPORTANT PEOPLE (NAMES, ADDRESSES, PHONE NUMBERS)

ACCOUNTANT _____

ATTORNEY _____

BANKER _____

CLERGY _____

EXECUTOR OF ESTATE _____

FINANCIAL PLANNER/CONSULTANT _____

INSURANCE AGENT(S) _____

INVESTMENT ADVISER(S)/STOCKBROKER(S) _____

PHYSICIAN(S) _____

OTHERS (Children's Guardians, etc.) _____

LOCATIONS: ORIGINAL WILL(S) _____ TRUST DOCUMENTS _____

SAFE DEPOSIT BOX _____ OTHER _____

SECTION II
Specific List of Insurance and Investments

INSURANCE POLICIES

NAME OF COMPANY	POLICY OR ACCT. #	PRODUCT NAME/TYPE	BENEFITS	CASH VALUES

INVESTMENTS

NAME OF COMPANY	ACCOUNT NUMBER	PRODUCT NAME/TYPE	BENEFITS	VALUE

PROPERTY

PROPERTY NAME/DESCRIPTION	LOCATION	VALUE

SECTION III
Assets, Liabilities & Net Worth

Name: _____ Date: _____

OWNERSHIP:	SELF	SPOUSE	JOINT	OTHER	TOTAL
ASSETS					
CASH/CHECKING					
SAVINGS ACCTS.					
MONEY MKT. FUNDS					
CDs					
STOCKS/BONDS					
MUTUAL FUNDS					
STOCK OPTIONS					
IRA ACCOUNT(S)					
KEOGH ACCOUNT(S)					
VESTED PENSION(S)					
EMPLOYER THRIFT					
LTD. PARTNERSHIPS					
ANNUITIES					
HOME					
OTHER REAL EST.					
PERSONAL PROPERTY					
LIFE INS. CASH VALUE					
BUSINESS INTERESTS					
OTHER					
TOTALS (A)					
LIABILITIES					
MORTGAGES					
PERSONAL NOTES					
CREDIT CARDS					
1)					
2)					
3)					
UNPAID TAXES					
TOTALS (B)					
NET WORTH (A) - (B)					

SECTION IV
Income Assessment

What is your annual income now? $_____

What will it likely be next year? $_____

In five years?   High $_____   Low $_____

In ten years?   High $_____   Low $_____

In twenty years?   High $_____   Low $_____

SECTION V
Financial Objectives

Name of Objective	Define Specifically	Target Date	Estimated Cost	Comments

SECTION VI

The 10% Solution
Your Ideal Budget Schematic

10% TITHE	10% SAVINGS, INVESTMENT & LIFE INSURANCE	10% CONTINGENCY	70% LIVING EXPENSE

YOUR LIVING EXPENSE BUDGET

ANNUAL   MONTHLY

Income (Fed., State & Local) & Soc. Sec. Taxes . $

Mortgage & Real Estate Taxes (or Rent) . . . . . . $

Food & Household . . . . $

Gas & Electric . . . . $

Other Utilities (Phone, water & sewer) . . . . $

Auto Payments . . . . $

Auto Escrow (For maintenance & repair) . . . . . $

Parking & Other Transportation . . . . $

Disability Insurance . . . . $

Auto & Home Insurance . . . . $

Clothing . . . . $

Recreation & Personal Gifts . . . . $

Vacation . . . . $

_____ . . . . $

_____ . . . . $

_____ . . . . $

Misc. . . . . $ _____ _____

Budget Objective . . . . $

SECTION VII
Basic Allocation Plan

ASSET ALLOCATION PLAN

	WHEN NEEDED?	EXISTING ALLOCATION	NEW ALLOCATION	TYPE OF FINANCIAL PRODUCT
CONTINGENCY, CASH/EMERGENCY				
HOUSE				
FOR NEXT CAR				
ESCROW ACCOUNTS				
LONG-TERM INVESTMENTS				

CASH FLOW ALLOCATION PLAN
(MONTHLY)

	WHEN NEEDED?	EXISTING ALLOCATION	NEW ALLOCATION	TYPE OF FINANCIAL PRODUCT
CONTINGENCY, CASH/EMERGENCY				
LIFE INSURANCE				
DISABILITY INS.				
FOR HOUSE				
FOR NEXT CAR				
ESCROW ACCOUNTS				
LONG-TERM INVESTMENTS				
TOTALS				

SECTION VIII
Action Plan

	OBJECTIVE DEFINED	DECISIONS MADE	ACTION TO TAKE	TARGET DATE	DATE IMPLE-MENTED
INSURANCE:					
DISABILITY INS.					
LIFE INSURANCE					
OTHER INSURANCE					
INVESTMENTS:					
CONTINGENCY FUNDS					
SHORT-TERM					
LONG-TERM					
ESTATE PLANNING					
TAX PLANNING:					

FOURTEEN

Implement Your Plan

B ob came to me five years ago for some planning advice. His goal was to take early retirement in ten years at age fifty-five and devote the rest of his life to full-time ministry. I spent time brainstorming and came up with recommendations that were within his budgeting capabilities and would give him a high probability of reaching his goal. It would take discipline, I told him, and it assumed there would be no emergencies that would require any of the assets or cash flow.

Five years later, it is clear that Bob will not reach his goal. While he is better off today, it would still take him over eight more years to be able to retire under his original objective. Why? Because he failed to implement the plan. Every time I called him, he would come up with another excuse.

"I need to think about it."

"I've been terribly busy lately, and I just haven't gotten around to studying it carefully."

"I had another broker call me, and he said I should do something else."

"Maybe we should get together again. It's been so long now, I'm not sure exactly what it was you recommended."

It's a shame, both for Bob and me. He will not realize his goals and will probably miss out on some rich blessings. Hours of my time went down the drain because he never implemented the plan.

How to Make Decisions and Act on Them

A large part of Bob's problem was procrastination. He had no real objections to my recommendations, and he admitted that they solved his problem. He just couldn't seem to take action.

If you have the tendency to procrastinate or have general difficulty making financial decisions, here are some suggestions to help you make decisions and act on them.

1) *Ask for help.* Find advisers you can trust, and ask them to let you know if they think you are procrastinating. Have your spouse or a friend hold you accountable for decisions you need to make.

2) *Set deadlines.* Once you have a reasonably sufficient amount of information with which to make a decision, put a date down in your calendar by which you will make a definite decision and take action. You owe this to yourself and the adviser(s) making the recommendation.

3) *Abide by the date,* treating it as a covenant. In your own mind, treat the decision as a very important, binding matter.

4) *Pray about it.* Ask God to give you wisdom. Ask Him for clarity and conviction. If, after all of the above, you cannot come up with clear reasons not to proceed, then make a positive decision to take the recommended action. If there are some good reasons to say no or to wait, voice them.

5) *If your decision is yes,* set a date for implementation, or do it right then and there if possible. Call your adviser, fill out forms, write a check, or take whatever other action is required. Stop talking and do.

6) If the decision is no, then make it emphatic to all involved. If it is something that is a no for now, but should be looked at again in the future, set a date now for review. Sometimes there are good reasons for waiting. By putting a time frame on the wait, you help yourself and your advisers avoid letting things fall through the cracks.

How to Avoid Mistakes

Everyone makes mistakes. What you want to do is avoid major ones and make fewer minor ones.

One very important safeguard is to use the unity principle I described in Chapter 7. Only make larger expenditures after you and your partner have talked it over and agree it is the right thing to do.

Another is to determine whether this action would violate any other sound financial principles or would impede any other more important financial goal. If you can't match it to a clear objective, or if it involves too much risk or will tie your money up too long, then you should probably decide against it.

Get advice from experts. If you are having doubts, run it by a professional or professionals you trust and who have demonstrated wisdom in the past.

As a final check, always ask if the proposed action violates any biblical principles. If it does, then avoid it.

How to Use Financial Professionals

In other chapters, particularly Chapters 8 and 12, I have discussed the need for professionals and the kinds of credentials and qualifications they should have. If you have found advisers who are competent and trustworthy, use them wisely; they are as important to your financial health as a good family doctor is to your physical health.

Most financial professionals want to do what is best for you. They also need to get paid. There will always be a temptation for both salespeople and fee-based advisers to make recommendations that will make them more money. Salespeople may be tempted to steer you to a product you don't really need because it pays higher commissions. A fee-based planner, accountant, or attorney may be tempted to make recommendations that will result in more "billable hours" for them.

You can help your adviser avoid such temptations by following a few basic principles. First, find out how the adviser will get paid. By discussing this up front, both you and the adviser have a chance to decide if the relationship will be mutually profitable.

Second, let your adviser know that if you are pleased with the work, you will do business with him or her, that you will be loyal on a long-term basis and will not create too much work for too little pay by always going to the competition or procrastinating.

Third, if the adviser is paid by commissions, ask the adviser to do any "shopping" for you and show you a few alternatives. If you are going to put your case out for competitive bidding, make that clear up front and let each adviser know by what criteria you will make your decision. That way they can decide whether it is worth doing the work.

Do not expect your adviser to be clairvoyant; if you have a question or a need, pick up the phone. I try to stay in touch with all my clients, but the ones who get the best work out of me are the ones who stay in touch with me on their own initiative.

Lastly, take the time to be knowledgeable. I truly believe that my best ally is a knowledgeable client. This person will be less likely to follow fads or fall for the overpromising sales hype with which the marketplace is inundated. If you are not willing to be a knowledgeable, involved client, then it is doubly important to be able to trust those with whom you do business.

How to Choose Financial Products

It is next to impossible to really "shop" by yourself for financial products. There are approximately 2600 different mutual funds from which to choose—more than the number of stocks on the New York Stock Exchange! There are thousands of insurance companies. Hundreds of banks and savings institutions are within a ten-mile radius of your home if you live in a city or suburb. It is impossible for even full-time professionals to keep up with all the options available.

Various companies use differing assumptions and product features. Consumer magazines and newspapers often publish incomplete, distorted, or erroneous information. In the early 80s, one popular magazine did an analysis of disability insurance and was forced to print a full-page retraction the following month because the information and conclusions were completely off base. Anyone following the magazine's advice could have made a serious, even catastrophic financial mistake. This is why it is important to employ full-time professionals who are intimate with the markets and trained to understand products.

If your planning indicates a need for a product category, such as life insurance or a growth mutual fund, first try to determine what varieties of that product are available through your adviser. Then narrow it down to two or three that meet the following criteria:

1) *Financial condition and reputation*—the company should have sufficient assets to back their product(s), should not have too much debt, should be highly rated according to industry standards, and should have a reputation for integrity and service.

2) *Track record*—the product or its sponsor should have both a short-term (one to five years) and a long-term (ten to twenty years) track record that is respectable by industry standards. For insurance, that would include a steady history of dividends and/or rates. For mutual funds, you would look at total return figures, net of expenses. For a stock, you would look at the management, debt, product mix, and position in its own market(s) among other things.

3) *Appropriateness and suitability*—try to narrow the choices to those products which come closest, in terms of design and composition, to the planning reasons that brought you to this product category, and which are suitable to your financial situation and risk tolerance.

4) *Price or current rates*—the price should be reasonable in light of expected performance, but do not sacrifice quality for price. Many people are overly influenced by rate quotes. When all else is equal, the best current rates can be used as tiebreakers.

5) *Special situations*—are there special situations that make this a particularly good buy at this time?

How to Set Up Self-fulfilling Plans

When possible, set up your plans so that they can run smoothly, minimize the dangers of forgetfulness, and do not require your constant attention. Whether you see it as "forced savings," a way to keep things simple and easy, or a way to avoid having to make too many decisions, such plans can make your finances run more smoothly and give you a greater chance to achieve your financial goals. A few ideas follow.

1) *Buy insurance with annual premiums or on an automatic checking withdrawal system.* You have to write fewer or no checks and therefore run less of a risk of a lapsed policy.

2) *Buy mutual funds on an automatic checking withdrawal system.* You will not have to remember to write checks and you will get the benefits of long-term, disciplined investing on a regular basis.

NOTE: If you use automatic checking withdrawal systems, you still need to make entries in your checkbook register and always keep enough money in your checking account to guard against insufficient funds charges.

3) *Use a cash management account* (money market fund) *with your broker for your investment accounts.* With such an account, you can buy stocks, bonds, CDs, and other products over the phone without having to fill out forms or leave your home or office. Dividends, interest, and other proceeds from investments can be automatically "swept" into your money fund and immediately start earning interest without your doing anything.

4) *Have distributions from one product automatically deposited into another.* Many investments and insurance products will allow you to direct distributions or dividends to go directly to another product. For instance, you could have distributions from a limited partnership received and deposited into a mutual fund, or dividends from one insurance policy directed to pay premiums on another. This is also an easy and effective way to achieve added diversification in your investment portfolio.

5) *Use payroll deduction plans.* Some employers offer options to buy financial products, including insurance and

401(k) savings plans through automatic payroll deductions.

Individual Exercise

Each write your own answers to the following questions.

• Do you procrastinate ____a lot ____a good bit ____somewhat ____very little ____not at all ____I'll answer this later

• Does your partner procrastinate ____a lot ____a good bit ____somewhat ____very little ____not at all

• What do you think would help you and/or your partner to procrastinate less?

• What financial decisions do you think you and your partner need to make over the next six months?

Discussion

Share and discuss your answers as you have done in previous chapters.

• After discussing the financial decisions you thought you would need to make over the next six months, write deadlines in your calendars, including dates to call any advisers with whom to set appointments. Decide which of you will do the calling.

FIFTEEN
Your Inheritance And Legacy

"Thus says the Lord, 'Set your house in order; for you shall die."
(II Kings 20:1)

Ted and Sheryl married when they were twenty-five years old and enjoyed a strong, loving relationship from the beginning. It had not been easy, especially in the early years as Ted struggled to get his computer supply business off the ground. But even through that stressful period and the challenges of raising four active children, their basic love and respect for each other remained firm.

After thirteen years, everything had fallen in place. Sheryl was at home, having left work to raise their family. They lived in a lovely neighborhood in one of the best school districts in their city. The business was successful and provided more income than they really needed. They were very involved in their church, and gave generously of their time, talent, and money to help others. With a good marriage, a beautiful home, healthy kids, a successful business, and a genuine commitment to Jesus Christ, they were the envy of many.

Then Ted was killed in a freak accident. Overnight, Camelot was brought to ruin. Like most of us, Ted and Sheryl never seriously imagined that God would allow them to die prematurely. They were too healthy, too young, and too involved in ministry. Because they never took the possibility seriously, they had not prepared for it in their financial plans.

They had bought $50,000 of life insurance on Ted about five years before, but had not seen the agent since. While Ted had bought some excellent health insurance for his three-person business, there was only $25,000 of group life insurance. There was no will, and Ted and Sheryl had never discussed funerals or the disposition of his business if he died.

Sheryl found herself and her children cast adrift on uncharted waters. The estate settlement process was long and unpleasant. All the assets, including the business, were added to the estate. It seemed to her that they had valued the business terribly high, but then she had never been very involved in it. Ted had always taken care of all the finances, saying he didn't want her to worry about those things.

It seemed like every time she turned around, somebody had a hand out: creditors, attorneys, courts, state tax collectors. The life insurance was not enough, so the executor had to invade savings accounts and retirement plans to pay both the personal and business creditors.

To make matters worse, the business began to go downhill. Sheryl tried to get involved and take over, but the one salesman was resentful, feeling he should now have the business. The secretary/receptionist was fine, but she couldn't work for free. The accountant and attorney were helpful, but their bills weren't. The insurance guy had finally shown up and proposed she buy a lot of insurance on herself to protect the kids, but the premiums were too high.

One year after Ted's death, the business was virtually dead. The salesman had left to start his own company, and was now taking accounts away from his former firm. Sheryl could not pay the secretary and have anything left to pay herself. While she had preserved most of their IRA accounts, all other savings and investments had been depleted, and she had collected more debts.

She was now faced with the prospect of having to let the business go and find a job. It was evident that she and the children could not afford to live in their house any longer. It was a cruel and desperate situation, and all the more discouraging because most of the financial disasters could have been avoided.

If they had done a careful analysis of their life insurance needs and bought enough while they could afford it, there could have been little or no problem with cash needs to pay the creditors and attorneys and tax people. Carefully written wills and/or a living trust and wise organization of asset ownership could have saved tens of thousands of dollars of probate costs and state inheritance taxes. A buy-sell agreement funded by life insurance could have allowed Ted's salesman to buy out Sheryl's interest in the business, while letting her receive some residual income from the company into which Ted had poured his creative talents and energy. She and the children did not have to face financial disaster.

If we could interview Ted now, I am sure he would tell us that this was not how he wanted himself to be remembered—as the great guy who failed to plan, and thus failed to take care of all that was dearest to him in the world.

Children of Promise

The centerpiece of the Old Testament economy was the land and the families to which it was given. This, along with their relationship to God, was their inheritance. The inheritance was the result of God's promise to Abraham and Moses. That is why it was called the Promised Land.

The worst thing that could happen to a Israelite, next to losing his relationship with God, was to lose his inheritance. He was a child of The Promise, and that promise was embodied in the land itself. Ownership of the inheritance was economic productivity and independence. It was economic security and honor. To lose the inheritance was to enter into bondage.

The Promise is a wonderful expression from God, and one that is not just an historical curiosity. The Promise embraces the past, present, and future simultaneously. It is past and present evidence of God's love and grace. It is also hope and confidence in the future. The Israelite taught his children about The Promise, and he passed the spiritual portion (the relationship) and the physical portion of it (the land) to them. This was the legacy of God's people, and as good stewards, they were to preserve and prosper it and pass it on to their children.

It is important for us to understand that God's great purpose is to redeem not only the people, but the creation itself. In this context we can begin to understand the fullness of what stewardship means. Stewardship is the redemption of and care for all of life and the creation in which it exists. Even evangelism is stewardship. There is no function of the church and its people that may escape from the steward's responsibility.

It is this awesome understanding of stewardship that is to be passed from generation to generation. All that we have learned and all that we have accumulated should be considered as a generation to generation responsibility. There are some who advocate leaving everything to ministry. I take serious issue with them. I am not aware of the people of Israel donating their inheritances to the priests. The priests and Levites were not to be owners because of their special position. The tithes were to be sufficient for them. The inheritance was to be kept along generational lines.

Therefore, while I recommend considering some charitable giving in an estate plan, and even giving all of the estate where there is no family, I believe the first consideration within the priorities of stewardship is to take care of your family.

What Will You Leave, and to Whom?

You may be thinking that you don't really have much. Perhaps you are just starting out. Life isn't too complicated, and you don't have kids yet. For you, this may be knowledge to be remembered for a later time.

However, I believe everyone should consider a few practical things. First of all, there are costs associated with dying. There are funeral and probate costs, and debts have to be paid. Even for someone who owns very little, the costs can be $10,000-$20,000. Do you want your spouse or parents or siblings to have to deal with that?

You also probably have personal property, some of which you might consider as sentimentally valuable to you and someone else. If you die without a plan, the government will make one for you. Do they know how you would like your property distributed? As God's steward, are you acting responsibly by abdicating these decisions to the government?

This is why I believe everyone, including newlyweds, ought to have a will, a trust, or an ownership arrangement which assures that their assets will be distributed according to their wishes. This is also an opportunity to leave a message of love for your spouse, your family and others, a testimony which can live on in the memories of those you leave behind.

How Do You Want to Be Remembered?

This is really the key question, isn't it? I imagine few of us would want to leave this world with people thinking how unprepared, inconsiderate, and irresponsible we were. We make an impact, both in life and death, in the way we live and in the way we die. If, in our deaths, we can verify and anchor that which we said and did in our lives, then we have a complete and powerful testimony to the world.

I think of Dawson Trautman, who founded the Navigators, a wonderful organization that emphasizes Bible study within strong personal and small-group relationships. While boating, a young girl fell overboard. Dawson dove in after her, found her, and struggled to get her back to the boat. When his companions had brought the girl safely into the boat, they turned to find that Dawson had disappeared under the water.

Why, we ask, would God allow this to happen to such a good servant when he had so many more years ahead of him? I don't know. What I do know is that here was a man of God who, in death, verified everything for which he had lived. He left both a spiritual and a physical legacy in the memories, in the lives of those he touched and in the organization which he founded.

Yes, we leave behind much more than just material possessions. There is a legacy of ideas and character, of memories and feelings, of belief and faith. No finite price tags can describe these.

Never believe that you can not make a significant difference in this world. That marvelous old film, *It's a Wonderful Life,* poignantly expressed this. Despairing of his life, and what he perceived as his abject failure, the character played by Jimmy Stewart is ready to jump off a bridge. Then an angel, disguised as an old man, shows him what the world would be like if he had never been born. He had saved his brother's life, made it possible for others to own their own homes, kept still others from financial disaster and personal sorrow and despair.

God will use you if you will let Him. Take your life and become a real steward of it. Give yourself to Jesus Christ, and ask Him to fill you with His love and His purpose. Follow His principles and teach them to your children and others. You will have a wonderful life and build a valuable legacy for those who come after you.

Individual Exercise

- What was "The Promise" to Israel and how do you think it applies to you?

- Thinking of your material assets, what would you want to happen to them if you died tomorrow? Are you sure that they would indeed be distributed in this way? (Refer to your net worth statement at the end of Chapter 13.)

- Is there a special message you would want to leave to your spouse? to your family? to others?

- How would you most like to be remembered?

Discussion

Share your answers to the above questions, without immediate comment or evaluation.

• Discuss your answers. How does your spouse's/fiance's answers make you feel? Are there any actions you should take now (e.g., see an attorney, financial planner, or life insurance agent)?

APPENDIX

Six Major Decisions to Talk about Now

1) *Where to live*

This decision is the biggest financial commitment (other than kids) that most people make. Many factors should be considered here, including the following: present and future income, your budget priorities, job stability, possible need to move within five years, taxes, future of area/location, future family, life-style versus saving and giving, God's will, rent or buy.

2) *What career(s)*

The key question for Christians is, "What is my special calling in life?" What does this say about our life-style, income, and costs we can expect to have? Whether your calling is to be a business owner/employer, a corporate executive, a teacher, or a missionary will require different types of financial decisions and commitments.

Will you need start-up capital? How much and where will it come from? How will this affect where you will live? What expenses can you forecast? Will this be temporary? God often has multiple callings for us, which may require numerous career changes. Or He can give you more than one calling at the same time. An example would be the business owner who also has a teaching ministry.

Avoid sacrificing your values, integrity, family and marriage just to "get ahead." "For what will it profit a man, if he gains the whole world and forfeits his life?" (Matthew 16:26)

3) *What about kids?*

In today's dollars, each child is about a $200,000 financial commitment over twenty or so years. (It can be a lot more.) If you are going to bring children into the world, begin to save and invest for them now. Sacrifice some of the luxuries and unnecessary fluff so you can develop good habits and values upon which to raise a family. How many children would you like to have? When do you want to have your first child? What kind of a family and life-style do you want them to have as they grow up? How do you think God would like you to answer these questions? Pray to Him for wisdom and guidance, for there is no greater human responsibility than to be a parent.

4) *Who will raise the kids?*

The balancing act of raising children and pursuing careers is difficult. Will one of you stay home, at least while your children are young? Will you make use of day-care, school, and sitters? Will it be okay to have "latchkey" children? What will be the roles of mother and father?

5) *What kind of car?*

This question relates to the others in terms of priorities and life-style commitments. Is it important to be able to cruise at 120 mph? Will you buy a car for status or for transportation? New or used? Will you finance it?

6) *What kind of life-style?*

There is no "right" answer here, and I would never presume to tell anyone else how to live in terms of material wealth and comfort. We must keep in mind, however, that the Bible warns those who are blessed with plenty that they are responsible for it and will give account to God for their stewardship. Even an average income in the United

States puts one in the top five percent of the world!

"Every one to whom much is given, of him will much be required." (Luke 12:48)

" . . . as you did it to one of the least of these my brethren, you did it to me." (Matthew 25:40)

"But if any one has the world's goods and sees his brother in need, yet closes his heart against him, how does God's love abide in him?" (I John 3:17)

"He who is kind to the poor lends to the Lord." (Proverbs 19:17)

Read Psalm 112. How can you live in such a way as to have the description of the blessed man apply to you?

Eleven Major Mistakes to Avoid

1) *Buying too much house*

Tell real estate agents that your price range is $45,000-50,000, and they will show you houses from $49,000 to $54,000. That's because they know that if they can get your desires at a high pitch, you will stretch yourself to get what you want. Rule of Thumb: Whatever you think it will cost, it will cost more—often ten to twenty percent more. Think about what would happen if you were fired or disabled and lost part or all of your income for a period of six months or more. If you stretch too far for housing, you could create a big financial problem.

2) *Buying too much car*

Just as with housing, many people stretch beyond their means to buy a car they really don't need. A new car costs the most to run during its first two to three years, when the fastest and most significant depreciation occurs, along with any financing payments. If you buy a new car every couple years, chances are you are wasting a lot of money. At best, status and luxury (as differentiated from quality) should be secondary motivations in choosing an automobile; at worst, they are unnecessary and sinful and will get you into trouble if you are not careful.

3) *Borrowing to buy consumer goods and accepting loans from "finance companies"*

Borrowing to purchase anything *except* that which has the probability of appreciating in value (i.e., a home or business) or of increasing your income (i.e., business vehicle) is unwise. Buying on time depreciating items is pure consumption at its worst. For instance, you can finance a stereo, take it out of the store, and owe more on it tomorrow than you could sell it for.

I cannot tell you the number of people I have talked to who got themselves into a debt problem and then compounded it by accepting a "consolidation" loan from a finance company. Typically, these people ran up thousands of dollars on credit cards and began to have problems keeping up all the payments. A finance company offered a consolidation loan with a lower, "affordable" monthly payment. Without really looking at the ramifications or the fine print, they accepted the loan only to find themselves deeper in the hole, because they would have to be paying two to three times as long—and at a twenty-two percent interest rate! And they could not pay it off early without a huge penalty. Avoid the usury of these parasitic enslavers like the plague.

4) *Being a spendthrift*

"Spendaholic" or "shopaholic" are relatively new terms for people who cannot go to a shopping mall without spending and overspending. If you are such an addicted spender, or even if you just have a compulsive streak from time to time, you must discuss it with your partner now and find a way to deal with it. Get professional counseling if you need it. Failure to curb uncontrolled spending is a serious threat to your marriage.

5) *Being "penny-wise but pound-foolish"*

Ironically, though, being too tight with money can be just as foolish and destructive as being too loose. Do not sacrifice quality for price. When you buy furniture, it is better to wait and save to buy a table that will last for generations than buy at a low price one that will break down within five years. Cheap is not a synonym for best. Appreciate and affirm quality workmanship and value; seek it out and be willing to pay a reasonable price.

6) *Ignoring estimated tax payments*

You should have a good idea of what you will owe in taxes at the beginning of the year. Go to the library and find the tax tables and forms or find someone to help you. Then make sure either your employer withholds enough or start a monthly escrow account (a passbook savings account designated "for taxes" will do). Forgetting about this or ignoring it too long has gotten many people into debt problems. The IRS is among the least forgiving of creditors; it has power to attach liens and seize property, among other things. Tax laws are an exceptional area of our legal system, where you can be presumed guilty until proven innocent. So render unto Caesar on time that which is his, and you will avoid some serious problems.

7) *Succumbing to greed and sales hype*

Greed is subtle. Like too much sun at the beginning of the summer, it can sneak up on us and burn us before we're aware of it. Often it is aided and abetted by sales hype. Insurance, investments, clothes, cars—nearly everything is sold with "hype," the slang abbreviation for "hyperbole," which means "exaggeration" or "overstatement."

Jeans don't keep us warm; they attract the opposite sex or give us social status. Toy commercials pack so much excitement and action into a thirty-second slot that kids are virtually salivating for something that will bore them after thirty minutes of actual play. Banks claim the greatest of altruistic motives for getting us to borrow all that money. Advertisers and salespeople have to fight for our attention in these ways only because it is what we respond to; the consumer is as much or more to blame as the marketers for the can-you-top-this hysteria.

The epitome of subtle greed is usually involved in the plethora of "get rich quick" schemes that surface every year. I am amazed at how many Christians get taken in by these. For instance, a few years ago I got quite a few calls from Christians who had gone to one of the late night TV real estate gurus. He had promised to make everyone a millionaire through buying real estate with "no money down," using OPM (Other People's Money).

I won't go into detail, but the essence of my response was that 1) if that was really the way to make money, why was the guy spending all his time traveling around giving seminars?, 2) the "OPM" was the money of the suckers that paid $450 a crack for the seminars and courses, and 3) some of the techniques advocated, such as obtaining fore-closed property from unfortunate and oppressed people, were not exactly loving and didn't stand up well against the biblical view of "just balances" and kindness to the poor and needy. Ironically, one of the leading promoters of these seminars went bankrupt and could not cover the thousands of requests for refunds.

Another place where I see motives getting confused is in multilevel marketing schemes. Pitches by promoters are often less concerned with the product or service than with recruiting another person to join the organization so they can build a pyramiding income under them. They lead with the marketing plan, not the product. High pressure and promises of great riches are the focus of the pitch, while the rationalization is that you will be helping others make money.

I am not saying multilevel marketing is wrong, but I do want to point out that, while legal, these plans are distant cousins to chain letters and "Ponzi schemes," pyramid plans requiring geometrically increasing numbers of players in which those in on the ground floor benefit the most and those getting in later end up with little, or, in the case of the illegal schemes, nothing.

Again, I am not saying all such marketing plans are bad. They can be very useful and legitimate methods for product distribution. I only want to call your attention to the fact that it is very easy to be persuaded for the wrong reasons. If you ever consider getting into such an organization, just make sure you have checked your motives and realize that those who are selling you the program rarely tell you the negative side and may have only their own welfare in mind.

Whether we are looking at ways to make money or ways to spend it, we need to develop a good sense of what is real and what is hype. A good rule of thumb: If it looks too good to be true, it probably is.

8) *Trapping yourself with insufficient liquidity*

Liquidity is the word used to describe the ability to convert an asset to cash and be able to use it immediately. The cash in your pocket or your checking account represents the highest degree of liquidity. Conversely, real estate, most limited partnerships, and privately held companies are not very liquid and take considerable time to convert to cash. Stocks traded on an exchange may be liquid, but you don't want to be forced to sell at an inopportune time.

In your planning, pay serious attention to your present and future cash needs, including emergency funds. Before locking up money for a long time, imagine what would happen if you needed money for an unplanned emergency. Anticipate cash needs and plan maturity dates for investments accordingly. If you have a lot of assets tied up in real estate, closely held companies, or partnerships, make sure you have plenty of life insurance and disability insurance to avoid forcing assets to be liquidated at a loss in the event of death or disability.

9) *Taking inappropriate risks*

Remember the axiom: The higher the return desired, the higher the risk assumed. Always ask, "What is the worst-case scenario here?" Identify your risk and ask yourself if it is wise. Remember that sneaky little devil called greed? But even if your motives are good, the risk can still be inappropriate.

10) *Assuming you will never be out of a job*

In the last ten to fifteen years, job permanence has decreased greatly. Whether through layoff, "early retirement," or voluntary career changes, periods of unemployment need to be considered in financial planning. It typically takes three to six months to find a new job, and can be longer, depending on the type of job and the condition of the economy at the time. Can you survive that long without going into debt? This relates to liquidity, overspending, and undersaving.

11) *Underinsuring your risks*

"It only happens to other people." Such an attitude, whether admitted or not, can result in tragedy. Ignorance of risk can be just as bad as a denial of it. Too many people are underinsured in key areas such as health, life, disability, and auto insurance. Make sure your agent/planner helps you do a thorough risk analysis, and purchase the insurance you need as soon as possible. Review your needs whenever your situation changes.

Some Helpful Tips

1. *When to shop*

Plan ahead. Anticipate your needs and research different brands, models, etc., and their price ranges so you can take advantage of true bargains and make purchases when items are in their most favorable price ranges.

ITEM	WHEN TO LOOK FOR BEST PRICES
Air conditioners	February, July, August
Appliances (general)	After Christmas, July, August
Appliances (major)	October, November
Art supplies	After Christmas
Auto accessories	May
Baby carriages	After Christmas, January
Baby clothes	March, August, off-season
Bathing suits	July, August (September at resorts)

Bedding	February, June
Bicycles	September
Blankets, quilts	November, December
Books	After Christmas, January
Boys' clothing (general)	June, off-season
Boys' suits and coats	November
Cars (new, outgoing models)	September, October
Cars (used)	February, November, December
Carpets/Rugs	After Christmas, January, August
Children's clothes	July, December
Children's shoes	March
China, glassware	January, February, September, October
Christmas cards, decorations	After-Christmas clearance sales, October
Cosmetics	August
Costume jewelry	After Christmas, January
Coats, hats	December
Curtains/drapes	February, August
Electric fans	August, September
Electronic equipment	July
Fabrics	April, June, September
Fall fashions	September
Fall/winter clothes (general)	October, after Christmas
Fishing equipment	October
Floor coverings	June
Fuel	July
Furniture (general)	After Christmas, January, February, July, October
Garden supplies	March
Garden equipment	September, October
Glassware, china	January, February, September, October
Handbags/pocketbooks	After Christmas, May, July
Hardware	September

Houses	November, December, January, February
Housewares	February, March
Hosiery	April
Ice Skates	March
Jewelry	May
Lamps	February, September
Laundry equipment	March
Lawn mowers	August, September
Linens	May
Lingerie	After Christmas, January, April, June, July, October, November
Luggage	March, May, July
Men's apparel (general)	February, June
Men's coats	August, November
Men's furnishings	December
Men's overcoats	After Christmas, January
Men's shirts, shoes	July
Outdoor Furniture	May, August, September
Paints	September preinventory sales, January
Radios	February
Resort/cruise wear	December
Rugs	After Christmas, January, May, July
School supplies	August, October
Shoes (general)	After Christmas, January, May, November, December
Silver	August, October
Silverware	February
Ski equipment	March
Sports equipment	February
Sportswear	February, May, July
Stereos	February
Storm windows	February
Summer clothes	July
Summer sports equipment	July

Tires	May, August
Toys	After Christmas, January, February
TV sets, VCRs	February, May
Warehouse sales	Periodic
White sales (sheets, towels, etc.)	January, August, November
Winter clothing	November
Women's coats	August, October
Women's shoes	March, June

2. *How to spot a real bargain*

To spot a real bargain, you must usually have some knowledge of the item/service, especially regarding quality and prices. It also helps to be aware of how goods and services are distributed.

For instance, a manufacturer may sell an item for $50 to a wholesaler, who then sells it at $65 to a retailer, who sells it to the public at a "retail price" of $110. The retailer may advertise a "sale price" of $99, which still leaves him with $34 with which to pay his overhead and make a profit.

Some items have wide margins (the difference in the wholesale price and the retail price) and some have thin margins. By getting familiar with the items and comparing prices of different stores, you can get a feel for what is a real sale and what is a normal markdown from a high retail price.

With items that are rarely on sale, a ten- to fifteen-percent savings may be an excellent buy. But if the normal price around town is ten percent off, you probably won't get a real bargain until the item is marked down twenty percent or more.

Clothing often has a high margin. Look for discount marketers or sales that are thirty to fifty percent off. Be patient and don't insist on being a trendsetter, and you will save a lot of money.

You should nearly always be able to buy a car for much less than the sticker price, saving up to twenty percent or more for new domestic cars. (Certain foreign and high status cars will sell at full price or even at a premium; it will be wise to avoid the status car, and only buy at full price if you are confident that extra quality is what you are buying.)

Buy food with coupons and by the case where case discounts are offered. Avoid specialty items and small packages for which you pay a premium.

Bids on houses should be at least ten to fifteen percent below the asking price in a buyer's market and five to ten percent if it is a seller's market. TVs and appliances should be considered at fifteen to thirty percent off or more.

Don't be afraid to negotiate. Even if an item is not on sale, make the proprietor an offer. The worst she can say is "no," and if she sees you turn to walk out the door, you just might hear her call you back to accept your offer or make a counteroffer. I got a lawn mower that was marked at ten percent off for almost twenty percent off by negotiating this way.

Do not neglect garage sales and other sources. Jill and I bought our first and only bed and chest set for seventy-five dollars in 1971. When we first looked at it, what we could see was filthy and in pieces. But we had no bed and thought that it ought to do for a few years, maybe. When we got all the pieces home, cleaned them up, and put the set together, what we found was a mahogany sleigh bed, chest of drawers, and vanity made in the 1800s or early 1900s and in excellent shape. It even had the original wrought-iron springs. These are valuable, solid pieces of furniture which are still going strong almost two decades later and could easily have another century or more of use ahead of them.

3. *How to eat well on a limited budget*

Americans tend to eat too much of the wrong things, which often are also the more expensive things. Educate yourself and make sure you consistently eat from the four basic food groups—fruits and vegetables, meats, bread/cereals, and milk products.

Processed foods are generally more expensive, and often much of the nutrition is lost—in other words, you get less real value for your money. For instance, if you buy frozen broccoli with cheese sauce, you will probably spend more and receive less nutritionally than if you buy fresh broccoli in season and melt your own cheese (or eliminate the cheese sauce altogether). With the frozen broccoli, you pay extra for packaging (box and boilable bag), you've added extra ingredients, including preservatives (i.e., salt), and you've paid someone else to make the sauce and put it together. The same is true with macaroni and cheese, spaghetti sauce, and many other dishes, which are relatively easy to make.

It's not that all processed foods are bad for you. It is just that the more you rely on them, the higher your food bill will be. The rule of thumb here is, the more steps done for you, the more expensive it will be. So consider convenience carefully, and be willing to put some effort into meal preparation, and you will stand to save a lot of money.

Look for sales and coupons. Buy in bulk, anticipating needs. When you find a great price, buy more and freeze it. Take a calculator with you and figure out which size actually has the better per unit price. For instance, the "new improved" larger size selling at $1.19 for ten ounces is 11.9 cents per ounce, while the old package was $.99 for nine ounces, or 11 cents per ounce. This may not seem like a lot, but with other products having similar differences and multiplying such differences over course of a year, such penny-pinching could save hundreds of dollars a year. Generally, the fancier the packaging, the more the cost.

Avoid spending on unnecessary and generally nonnutritious items like sweets and chocolate milk. Buy less expensive cuts of meat and make them more tender by proper cooking techniques. Emphasize good fish and poultry instead of expensive cuts of meat. Buy fruits and vegetables in season.

If you have land, time, and a green thumb, grow your own food and freeze it. Don't overload plates—Americans generally consume more than is actually needed, hence we tend to be overweight. Eat healthy snacks—fresh fruit instead of cookies and chocolates. Don't buy nonfood items (cosmetics, etc.) in grocery stores; they are generally priced higher than at discount drugstores.

If you don't know what is a good diet, you can obtain information from the American Heart Association, libraries, some food companies, and even government agencies.

Always shop with a list, and avoid impulse spending on items not on the list. Don't shop for food when you are hungry; you'll buy more.

Finally, don't eat out, except for special occasions. Eating out should be a treat, not a regular habit. One dinner out can cost the same as it does to feed a family for a week at home. Pack lunches instead of eating at restaurants every day.

Prices can vary around the country, but a family should be able to eat good, nutritious meals as well as provide napkins, light bulbs, and most other household items for under $100 per month per person (1988 dollars). In other words, a family of four could have a monthly food and household budget of $400 or less, and eat very well.

4. *How to buy a car*
   NEW CARS
   The key rule here is to shop before you go to the showroom. This will help you to avoid getting carried away by sales hype and making an impulsive decision. Determine your price range in light of your budget and asset management constraints. Decide what general type of vehicle would make the most sense for you, considering both business and personal use. Research various models using information provided by publications such as Consumer Reports. Call the Better Business Bureau and other consumer groups to see if there have been a large number of complaints involving the cars you are considering.

Determine the base "dealer cost." Through Consumer Reports, for a modest fee, you can get an updated computer readout listing the dealer cost of the base car and the options for virtually any make and model.

Make a list of the make, model, and options that you want. Go to a few dealers and see if they have the exact vehicle or can order it. Make an offer, starting about one or two percent above the "dealer cost" figures. Such a price will often be acceptable to a dealer on most domestic cars, especially if there is a large inventory or the particular car has a greater supply than demand.

Shop enough in advance so you can order a car and wait for delivery. Don't buy a new car off the lot unless it exactly meets your specifications. Otherwise, you will probably spend more than you planned because dealer-ordered cars tend to be "loaded" with extras you probably don't need.

If the dealer balks at your offer, smile, say "thank you," and walk out the door to try another dealer. You just may hear the salesman call you back to let him "talk to the manager" and work something out. If you get a counter-offer, you can use it to see if another dealer will make a better one.

Because cars are such a big expense, and dickering is the accepted way of doing this kind of business, I believe it is appropriate to be an astute, hard-nosed "horse trader." It is right and fair that the dealer and salespeople make money, so you don't want to be too chintzy, but neither do you want to pay more than you should. Discounts will vary, but rarely should you pay full sticker price for a new car.

I also believe you should negotiate the selling price without consideration of a trade-in. Trade-in values are where many dealers can push the deal to their favor. Find what the wholesale and retail "book" prices are for your old car before you start bargaining. Often, your car insurance agent will be able to supply you with these facts. That way you can have the option to trade or sell the car yourself if the dealer is not giving you a fair value.

One final point to consider. As in most large, mechanical items, dealer service and reputation are important and should be the difference in any close decisions. It may be worth paying a little more if you will get better service over the long haul.

USED CARS

The same basic approach can be applied to used cars, except it is a bit trickier to identify true price ranges. "Book" price and condition are the two leading bench marks. Also, check *Consumer Reports* for their used-car issues. They have ratings based on repair costs, safety records, etc.

Once you think you've found a car you like, hire an independent mechanic to look it over and give an educated opinion as to the mechanical condition. If it checks out okay, make an offer that is reasonable, given the book price ranges. In most cases the dealer has built some "dickering room" into his asking price, so you should rarely pay the sticker price.

5. *How to buy a house*

To stay in control, use "The Ten Percent Solution" cash flow allocation guide. Do a detailed five-year budget plan. Out of your living expenses, identify a monthly housing expense budget. For most people, I recommend a monthly payment, including mortgage, property taxes, and insurance, of between twenty-five and thirty-five percent maximum of after-tax and after-tithe income. Also, remember to include such things as points, attorney's fees, moving, fix-up, and decorating costs into your down payment. As a general indicator, add another ten percent of the selling price to your down payment. Bank "points" or "loan origination" charges will amount to three to five percent of the amount borrowed, and you will probably need every bit of what is left over for moving expenses, curtains, and the rest. Do your budget before you start looking, and stick to it.

Research neighborhoods, school systems, taxes, etc., before you start actually looking at homes. Research both the asking prices in a neighborhood and the actual selling prices (these can be found in newspapers and real estate publications, as well as at city or county courthouse or record offices).

Know what your absolute maximum price is and agree to stick to it. Tell your real estate agent you are looking for homes in a range ten to twenty percent less than your maximum. Draw up a list of specifications to help the agent narrow down the choices.

If you think you have found the house you want, but are not sure of the actual value, have an independent appraiser look at the house. It can also pay to have people experienced with plumbing, electrical circuitry, and home building/remodeling inspect the house for hidden defects.

Once you have accounted for any defects and have a good idea of what the house is worth compared to other similar properties, you are ready to make a bid. Pick a number you think is fair, and make your bid.

Generally, you should be able to purchase a house for less than the asking price, except in a high-demand area where more than one buyer may be bidding at the same time. Start the bidding at least five percent under the asking price. I usually recommend starting at a ten percent discount. If interest rates are high and/or the area is in recession, the opening bid could probably be less.

Here is where you can also use the bidding process as a sort of financial "fleece." If God does not want you to buy the house, ask Him to show you by having the seller refuse to sell at the price you believe to be right. Pick your number and stick by it.

One of the best ways to get into home ownership is to be willing to buy an older home that needs some fixing. Sweat equity is how we bought our first home, and it was one of the smartest things we did as a young couple. Be willing to do some work and to wait for your "dream house."

For information about Mr. Weisbrod's ministry
(speakers, seminars, newsletter), write to:
Pittsburgh Publishing & Comm.
P. O. Box 15080
Pittsburgh, PA 15237

If you have found this book helpful and would like to help other couples become one financially, consider the following:

• Give *Becoming One Financially* as an engagement or wedding gift.

• Give a copy to your clergy and suggest that they use *Becoming One Financially* as a premarital and marital counseling tool.

• Convince your church to provide a copy for every couple who gets married in your church.

You can order copies of *Becoming One Financially* from your local bookstore or from the above address.